THE MAGICAL BATTLE OF BRITAIN

THE WAR LETTERS OF DION FORTUNE
EDITED BY GARETH KNIGHT

SKYLIGHT
PRESS

© The Society of the Inner Light, 1993, 2012
© Gareth Knight, 1993, 2012

This edition published in Great Britain in 2012 by Skylight Press,
210 Brooklyn Road, Cheltenham, Glos GL51 8EA

First published in Great Britain in 1993 by Golden Gates Press, Bradford on
Avon, Wiltshire.

Designed and typeset by Rebsie Fairholm
Publisher: Daniel Staniforth
Cover photograph by Matt Baldwin-Ives

Typeset in Minion Pro; titles are set in P22 Underground, a licensed digital
recreation of the London Underground lettering designed by Edward Johnston
in 1915.

Printed and bound in Great Britain by Lightning Source, Milton Keynes

British Library Cataloguing in Publication Data.
A catalogue record for this book is available from the British Library.

www.skylightpress.co.uk

ISBN 978-1-908011-45-9

CONTENTS

INTRODUCTION
Gareth Knight

DION FORTUNE AND THE WAY AHEAD

DION FORTUNE was a remarkable woman in many ways, a pioneering type, of whom it may be said not only that she lived before her time but that she did much to shape the times that came after her.

Born in Llandudno in North Wales in 1890, by her early twenties, despite no great formal education, she had become a psychotherapist at a leading clinic.

This was in a pre-First World War London, when horse drawn buses still plied the streets, and when the psychoanalytic discoveries of Sigmund Freud were beginning to take the world by storm. With his theories of the subconscious, and the importance of dreams, and the role of the suppressed sexual libido of everyday life, a whole new approach to the human mind was being born.

But revolutionary as these psychological theories were, Dion Fortune felt they did not go far enough to explain some of the hidden powers and secrets of the mind. She had stumbled almost by accident upon the powers of telepathy, which she found to be demonstrable within herself.

This came about in a wholly unexpected and coincidental way. She used to attend a local Theosophical Society meeting house for the simple if lowly reason that it was near her clinic and had good catering facilities. It was thus a convenient place to lunch. One day, almost in a spirit of jest, she stayed on for one of the lecture demonstrations, and discovered to her amazement that she was picking up the images that the lecturer was projecting in a simple experiment in telepathy.

This first-hand evidence could not be ignored, nor could it be explained by any of the current theories of psychology. So she made a point of looking out for unusual conditions of the mind that even the new psychoanalysis could not account for.

In this she was helped by meeting a Dr Theodore Moriarty, who knew a great deal about occult phenomena and its therapeutic possibilities.

The bonds of convention were, in the mean time, tightening. The British Medical Association ruled that only qualified medical practitioners should be recognised as analysts. This squeezed Dion Fortune out of her practice, but the war came along anyway, and in common with thousands of other women of the time she aided the national war effort by working on the land, to help make the country self-sufficient for food in a time of blockade. At a later stage of the war she helped conduct research into the use of soya as an alternative to meat.

She continued working with Moriarty, and what she learned and experienced from their association she wrote up in fictional form as *The Secrets of Dr Taverner*. Dr Taverner is loosely based on Moriarty, and an approach to psychic or psychological disturbances that goes beyond the current theory and practice of psychological and medical science.

This included the use of hypnosis, reading the state of the aura, reference to past incarnations – very fringe methods indeed medically speaking – to cope with various obsessions, suicidal tendencies, or apparent split personalities.

Dion Fortune claimed that although some of the stories might seem unbelievable, or to have been written up for dramatic effect, she had in fact felt it necessary to tone down some of the factual circumstances to make them fit for general publication.

However, as her knowledge of the deeper side of the mind progressed, so she moved away from abuse and pathology toward the more positive realm, of personal fulfilment, self improvement and spiritual enlightenment. To this end, like the analytical psychologist C.G. Jung, she studied spiritual traditions from many parts of the world, including the myths and legends of the ancient world, and discarded and outmoded sciences such as magic and alchemy.

She also studied under different contemporary teachers, seeking anywhere that might give her knowledge of the powers of the human mind. This included membership of a famous occult society, the Hermetic Order of the Golden Dawn, that attracted many notable personalities of the time, particularly from the world of the arts. These included the poet W.B. Yeats, the novelists Brodie Innes and Charles Williams, the children's writer Edith Nesbit, and a director of the Tate Gallery, Sir Gerald Kelly. She studied directly under Moina Macgregor Mathers, the wife of its principal founder, and a sister of the philosopher Henri Bergson.

But as she progressed further in her quest so she found that powers were awakening within her own mind. She seemed to be recovering what appeared to be memories of past lives, with their ancient wisdom. In the process she taught herself the techniques of trance mediumship, for she was no believer in relying upon the psychic powers of others.

All this led to her deciding to form her own group and teaching centre. Initially called the Community of the Inner Light, it later expanded into a Fraternity and then into a Society, and has proved to be a source of inspiration and guidance to sincere seekers ever since. An impressive roll of occult writers and teachers have since passed through its portals.

The Community's first base was at Glastonbury, towards which Dion Fortune was always strongly attracted. By one of those strange synchronicities that occur when someone is about to find their true life's work or destiny she was offered a plot of land at the foot of Glastonbury Tor, on the actual holy hill itself, and a government surplus army hut to put on it!

Soon she was established on the Tor, on the holiest earth in England, and a group of small chalets was built within the enclosed garden to accommodate students and kindred spirits.

Three strands of interest attracted her to Glastonbury and they remained the core of her teaching and life's work.

One was the Arthurian legend, and the Knights of the Round Table, which includes the Quest of the Holy Grail. Second was the mystical ambience of the place, as the site of the first Christian church in England. And third was the elemental significance of the earth itself, for Glastonbury is a site of ancient powers that go back far beyond recorded history, as the remains of a spiral trackway up the Tor to the standing tower suggest.

Glastonbury is full of associations of King Arthur. Some associate it with Camelot, the King's great palace. Others, more mystically, see it as the Isle of Avalon, from which the "once and future king" will one day return to save his country and people. In the middle ages, the tomb of King Arthur and Queen Guinevere, complete with lock of yellow hair, were found before the high altar of the abbey, on a plot still marked in the green sward.

The full range of Arthurian annals was exploited by Marion Zimmer Bradley in her epic novel *The Mists of Avalon*, drawing upon traditions also expounded by Dion Fortune, concerning Merlin, Morgan le Fay, the Lady of the Lake and other characters of ancient legend. Also John Cowper Powys' monumental novel, *A Glastonbury Romance*.

On the mystical side, Dion Fortune loved the abbey, once the finest in England, but now no more than a ruin, desecrated by King Henry VIII who also martyred its abbot. It still retains a grand magnificence from those of its walls still standing. Not only is it a place of profound peace and harmony but the veil is thin, not only to the spiritual world but to the psychic as well. It was here that a contemporary of Dion

Fortune, a qualified archeologist, Frederick Bligh Bond, discovered hitherto unknown parts of the structure buried beneath the ground. He made these discoveries through being guided by the automatic writing of a psychic friend, apparently from medieval monks who had lived and worshipped there. What they revealed turned out to be true, and a new chapel was found when diggings were made. The church authorities however could not come to terms with this psychic means of archaeological investigation, and despite his record of success Bligh Bond's services were terminated.

Dion Fortune linked the Christian mystical tradition and the Arthurian at her London headquarters, which she set up a few years later as her society grew in numbers. She established public services wherein the Holy Grail was a major part of the ceremony. It was visualised as a cup of inspiration hovering over the heads of the celebrants, thus linking a powerful form of mind working, concerted meditation upon evocative and sacred images, with conventional forms of worship.

The third aspect of Dion Fortune's work had to do with the elemental powers of nature, that can be channelled through ancient sacred centres and the "ley lines" that run between them. Glastonbury is associated with such traditions from early times. According to some, it is the centre of a gigantic prehistoric earthwork, and the surrounding streams, field boundaries, roads and other topographical features, if traced out, reveal a great primaeval zodiac. The sixteenth century magician Dr John Dee, a confidant of Queen Elizabeth I, is recorded as having investigated Glastonbury on these grounds.

Dion Fortune was one of the first to take the idea of ley lines and power centres seriously. This is not surprising if she situated herself at the centre of one. In fact much of what might be called the three fold strand of tradition to be found in the work of Dion Fortune is to be found in Glastonbury itself.

The books she wrote on the subject have guided many along this threefold way. One of her earliest was called *Sane Occultism* and this was the key-note to her whole outlook and approach. Her commonsense method of systematic training in the development of higher consciousness used Western rather than oriental traditions. These are represented by *The Esoteric Orders and their Work* and *The Training and Work of an Initiate*. And for serious students of symbolism she wrote the first readily understandable book on the subject, *The Mystical Qabalah*, in which she explains in simple terms the Tree of Life, which is the ground plan upon which much of western traditions are based, or what Dion Fortune called "the yoga of the west".

She was also a novelist of some skill, and used fiction to teach the practice of her theoretical principles. Although, understandably, they have not hit the "top best seller" lists, being for a discerning rather than a general public, they have continued in print in edition after edition for over half a century. Her last three are considered to be her best, *The Winged Bull*, *The Sea Priestess* and *Moon Magic*.

And still more of her work is now coming to light. Of particular interest are her weekly letters to students produced from 1939 to 1942 in the early years of the Second World War. These reveal much of what had hitherto remained secret of some of the techniques of mind working that she had developed over the years. In the crisis of confrontation with the evils of Hitler's Germany, when England stood for a time alone against the Axis powers, she helped to maintain the strength and resilience of the group mind of the nation by the evocation of relevant symbolism.

Such work is never entirely subjective. Our thoughts and feelings can be as powerful for good or evil as our physical actions, if the right techniques are used. This is why some of the practical applications of occultism have always been closely guarded and revealed only to tried and trusted students.

Dion Fortune regarded herself as very much a woman of the future. She held much the same high vision of her fraternity.

This she spells out in one of her monthly letters of 1943 in an article called "The Work That Lies Ahead". This was a view evidently shared by the readers of her letters, as the copy I have before me has been underlined by its recipient in the part italicised below.

> "Our position as a Fraternity is a unique one. We are of the world, but not in it. We cannot be otherwise than a part of our race and age as long as we are inhabiting time and space; yet, mentally, *those who accept the viewpoint of the Fraternity, and have been trained in its discipline until that viewpoint guides their lives, are no part of the age in which they live, but of an age that is yet to come.*"

Well, we are now some seventy years on from when this was written and it is perhaps possible to take a longer view of these claims and aspirations. One good way is to study these weekly, and later monthly, letters. They are virtually the casebook of a working occultist at a time of national and indeed world crisis, when the barriers of confidentiality were down in the urgency of the hour.

One thing that clearly comes across is her faith in her task and her destiny and the cause she served, in her characteristic commonsense and practical way. The esoteric principles which she had learned, and which she taught, stood her in good stead in this time of testing.

"Life may be difficult," she writes, "but it is not bewildering. Meanwhile we have to endure." And it is this firm vision and practical leadership that inspired those who gathered round her.

Practicalities had to come first, coping with the dispersal of the members of the Fraternity, precautions for the air raids, and the aftermath of the bombing. "The war has to be fought and won on the physical plane," she says, "before physical manifestation can be given to the archetypal ideals which with every week that passes are coming more clearly into view." But it is these archetypal ideals that are the province of the working occultist, and the formulation and dissemination of these in the early days of the war were very much part of Dion Fortune's practical task.

As she recalls: "Those who received this Letter when it was a Weekly Letter, written almost without exception with enemy planes overhead, and sent out in order to hold the Fraternity together during the dark days of the Blitz, will remember that it shadowed forth those ideals which today are rapidly assuming form as ideas in every man's mind."

Those ideals, in their archetypal form, and their mode of realisation, may now be read at leisure in the extracts from her letters that follow.

Those were heady and unusual times. Exceptional circumstances calling for exceptional remedies. "Those who were with us in those days," she recalls, "will remember how we opened our doors and welcomed all who would sit in meditation with us and taught them the esoteric methods of mind-working that had never been revealed before outside the Veil of the Mysteries, and that this work was done with a view to bringing into manifestation those very ideas that are now manifesting. What part we played in their manifestation we cannot know; but we do know that whereas then the Fraternity was a voice crying in the wilderness, the cry has now become a chorus."

These ideas are those that shaped the pattern of post-war social change and reconstruction, from the foundation of a welfare state to the reconstruction of the League of Nations. Britain was seething with such ideas at the time she writes, when the tide of the war had turned, to allow visions of the future beyond those of mere survival. At a particular level of realisation all such ideas have to be translated from archetypal ideals into practical politics, and it is here that the work of the occultist stops.

"The archetypes that we worked to bring into manifestation as seed ideas in the group mind of the race have struck root and are beginning to show above the soil," she continues. "Our task in this matter is therefore finished, for it is no part of our work, in fact it is expressly forbidden to us, to come down into the arena of politics. Our work in this direction is therefore done. What was sown will grow and bear seed. It is out of our hands now. The ideals have been worked out as ideas, and the ideas will be hammered into shape as policies, and the policies will be driven through in the face of the inertia and self interest always opposed to the growth of life, on whatever plane."

Practical realisation always results in some measure of shabby or expedient compromise. Much the same was found after the previous Great Fire of London, of 1666, when the vision of Sir Christopher Wren (whom Dion Fortune cites more than once) was frustrated in the building of a new city. And after the second world war, even what vision Wren had achieved in the skyline of London was further blighted by similar forces, combined opportunism and vested interest throwing up their glass and concrete towers of corporate hubris.

Sustained with the optimism of faith in God and the driving force of spiritual evolution, Dion Fortune was prepared to take the longer view in her expectations of the manifestation of the vision splendid, which "will come to pass with the passage of time, perhaps sooner, perhaps later, but with absolute certainty, because 'He will turn and overturn till he whose right it is shall reign.'"

This attitude of faith bears witness to her personally long proven experience of working with those she called the Masters. These contacts, which she had developed as early as 1922, and probably before, evince a deeper level of realisation and wisdom than is the general run of what is latterly called "channelling". Some examples will be found in the letters that follow, and their tone is characterised by the response to an understandably anxious question as to when the war was likely to end.

The reply was: "I cannot tell you when it will end, but I can tell you how it will end. When the conditions that gave rise to it have been worked out, it will end."

Far from being an evasion of the direct question as to a definite date in time, this response comes from outside of our normal perception of events and of time. The events in the outer world are seen firmly as the expression of the consciousness and state of soul of contemporary man. In other words, circumstances reflect consciousness. And this applies to individuals as well as to groups. An elementary but often difficult realisation for the general occult student.

Dion Fortune goes on to say, ostensibly in her own words, although the tone bears the hallmarks of direct quotation from her source of inner wisdom: "The causes that gave rise to the war lie deeper than the will to power of one man, or even of a nation; they lie in the souls of the mass of mankind – in the attitude towards life and standards of conduct of the innumerable individuals that make up the mass of the democratic as well as the totalitarian countries, for there is no such thing as a mass apart from the units that compose it. Lessons have to be learnt, lessons in the art of living and the process of evolution, and individuals have to change until the mass is leavened."

This throws an interesting light on the radical changes that are and have been taking place in the modern world, and which seem to have gathered pace as human realisations have responded to the ease of modern communication; when wars and the results of wars are shown within the hour on home television screens worldwide, not filtered through the cold print of journalistic despatches, days or weeks after the event. It may also demonstrate the importance of the less noticeable esoteric work of those who have their mental antennae attuned to the inner world of ideals and ideas. Their long term result lies in the climate of public opinion, of which even the most despotic of rulers are keen to take account.

And what of the future of her group, Dion Fortune asks, and describes it as "a small, carefully selected and highly trained group of people, dedicated to the service of the race and the study of the wisdom that enables them the better to serve God and Man."

She summarises its achievement. "Through the course of long years of laborious work, with little enough to show for it in the eyes of men, a channel of communication between the physical plane and the inner planes has been opened which enables those who use it to come and go in a way little realised by anyone who has not had experience of the higher grades of the Mystery Tradition."

"What use is to be made of this instrument?" she wonders, but gives no immediate or specific answer. For the Path of the Mysteries, whether that of an individual or that of a group, is ever the choice and the taking of the very next step. As in mountaineering, however high the intention and the vision, the way to get there is a matter of one firm hand or foothold at a time.

However, in the seventy years that have since elapsed, apart from whatever may have been achieved in seeding human consciousness as a whole with spiritual ideals, her Fraternity, or Society as it was later to be known to the outer world, has played an important function in the teaching of the teachers of another generation. Many of the familiar names on esoteric bookshelves have served some form of apprenticeship in the Society of the Inner Light, or otherwise come under its influence, at first or second hand. To say nothing of the important work of those who never bothered to get into print.

Much of this has been achieved by the process of "seeding". The "inner light" has spread from source (itself a ray from a "golden dawn"), to torch of learning, candle of vision, and sanctuary lamp on individual shrines in many diverse ways. And gone are the days when any splitting off from a parent group is seen only in terms of failure, betrayal or schism. More is it a question of the spreading of "dandelion clocks" of wisdom and experience, floating abroad on the four winds, to grow anew.

Whether one wishes to put the popular epithet "Aquarian" to it, the modern way is much more open. This is not merely an aftermath of the sixties revolution, but the wider, deeper, process of what has been called "the Externalisation of the Hierarchy." Not that the days of the enclosed formal group are a thing of the past. But certainly the choice for the seeker is a much more open and broader one than ever in the past.

Now, with the publication of these letters, at least in part, the task of those who run the plethora of informal, less structured groups on a more or less informal basis, or ad hoc workshops, sometimes to a surprising degree of power, can read how one of the old school, when confronted with abnormal circumstances, coped with running an extended and informally structured meditation group capable of becoming a formidable force in the group soul of the nation.

Also, in its week by week record in the earlier stages of the war, we have before us a chapter in the autobiography of a working occultist. And to some extent this may give the lie to the assumptions held in some quarters that by this time Dion Fortune had in any way fallen away from her life-long views and contacts. She is shown in these letters as a very capable, commonsense, and courageous leader, over a broad front of mystical, mythological and hermetic channels of evocation, at a particularly difficult time.

The weekly open meditation work was eventually discontinued, "not because it was unsatisfactory, but because it had developed to such an extent that it had become unwieldy. Not only had the numbers participating increased beyond all expectation, but the work had developed a degree of power that made it no longer possible to maintain an ever open door."

This is a problem (of success) that will be familiar to a number of modern teachers and facilitators. The very nature of the Mysteries, beyond a mere philosophical interest, imposes a certain graded structure, for some are capable of contacting and sustaining more powerful inner dynamics than others. This is largely a matter of training and experience. As Dion Fortune succinctly puts it: "Outsiders who came in at the beginning grew with the work, but once the work had developed in the way it did, it was no longer possible to take in outsiders."

Dion Fortune's solution to this problem was to close the doors to all but those who were prepared to undergo formal preliminary training. Nowadays, much of that preliminary training has come into the public domain. And this largely through the efforts and offices of those who passed at one time or another through the portal of the Mysteries under the guidance of Dion Fortune. In the letters that follow, a revealing chink is made in the Veil that guards that portal, enabling us to see at first hand something of the work that went on within, in those days of a previous generation of adepts and initiates of the Western Esoteric Tradition. It will be seen that the ideals and the practicalities remain the same.

Gareth Knight

THE WEEKLY LETTERS
With commentary by Gareth Knight

The Weekly Letters of Dion Fortune constitute an important part of her life's work, and are historically important in that they demonstrate a method of magical working using national and racial archetypes. Except for the conditions of war, they would have been reserved to the inner circle of senior initiates in her occult group, but with members dispersed, and meetings difficult because of air raids and travelling restrictions, the circulation of weekly letters to a wider circle of associates was deemed to be a way of keeping the work of the group going.

Hitherto, Dion Fortune's writings, and this includes such important works as *The Mystical Qabalah*, had appeared in the Society of the Inner Light's magazine, which had been running since 1927. This ceased publication in August 1940 but the Weekly Letters continued. The rationing of paper did not allow both publications to survive and the Letters were obviously held to be more important. They continued until the end of 1942 when, the severity of the immediate national crisis being over, they were replaced by a Monthly Letter.

The practical importance attached to the Weekly Letters is best illustrated by the preliminary document which was sent out at the beginning of October 1939, just one month after the outbreak of war. It was headed "Meditation Instructions" and gave details of how the subsequent letters were to be treated. It is worth reproducing in full, for it contains excellent instruction on meditation techniques.

MEDITATION INSTRUCTIONS

The members of the Fraternity of the Inner Light have been carefully trained in the theory and practice of meditation. Every Sunday morning from 12.15 to 12.30 certain members will hold a meditation circle in the Sanctuary at 3 Queensborough Terrace. Other members, scattered all over the country, will also sit in meditation at the same time. Thus a nucleus of trained minds will be formed.

All who care to join in this work are invited to participate. They should proceed as follows:

The weekly letters will be sent every Wednesday in order to ensure the punctual arrival in time for the following Sunday. On that day, but not before, study the contents of the letter in preparation for the united meditation at 12.15. It is inadvisable to study the papers sooner than this, lest the concentration on the previous week's work be disturbed. Success can only be achieved by single-pointed concentration.

The meditation work consists of certain well-defined stages, each of which must be carefully performed before passing on to the next. These stages are the steps of a stair on which the mind rises to a higher level of consciousness, performs certain work there, and then returns to normal. For convenience sake they are numbered in sequence.

Stage 1

Having studied the letter, take your seat if possible in a quiet, dimly lit room, secure from disturbance; face towards London; sit in such an attitude that your feet are together and your hands clasped, thus making a closed circuit of yourself. Your hands should rest on the weekly letter lying on your lap, for these letters will be consecrated before they are sent out in order that they may form a link. Breathe as slowly as you can without strain, making a slight pause at the beginning and ending of each breath, thus: breathe in, pause; breathe out, pause. The attitude should be poised and free from all strain, either sitting or lying. If sitting, have some support for the back. The position should be symmetrical so that both sides of the body are the same. It should be taken up a few minutes before the meditation is due to start, so that you have time to settle down into a posture of balanced relaxation and stabilise your breathing. Once the meditation has begun, think no more about your breathing.

Stage 2

Commence your meditation by thinking about the subject allotted for the work of the week. Try and realise its spiritual implications but do not attempt to consider its practical ones, for this will distract you and cause mind-wandering. Realise that ethical principles are involved. If you have any knowledge of the Qabalistic method, place your meditation on the Tree.

Stage 3

Having thoroughly filled your mind with the ideas set for the meditation work, picture in your imagination a symbolic image, figure or scene that shall symbolise it. Keeping this before your mind's eye, slow down your thought processes till you begin to "feel" rather than reason. Try, as it were, to "listen" mentally. Do not try to hold this mental stillness for more than a few moments, even if you feel you are getting results, because it is a very potent method of mind-working and it is not good to do it for long at a time. However fascinating you may find it, discipline yourself to pass on firmly to the next stage, for it is here that the real work is done.

Stage 4
Mentally dedicate yourself in the Name of the All-Good to the service of the One Life without distinction of friend or foe; let the good that you are about to invoke come through for all, relying upon the Cosmic Law to adapt it to their needs or their healing.

Stage 5
Think of yourself as a part of the Group-soul of your race; your life a part of its life, and its life the basis of yours. Then, invoking the Name of God, open your mind as a channel for the work of the Masters of Wisdom.

Stage 6
Meditate again on the subject set for the work of the week.

Stage 7
At the conclusion, say aloud: "It is finished". Imagine a pair of black velvet curtains being drawn across the scene you have built up in your imagination, as if it were on a stage. Let the curtains approach from either side till they meet in the middle, thus blotting out the scene. Rise from your seat and stamp your foot firmly on the ground to affirm your return to normal consciousness.

You must be careful to always "close down" after meditation, otherwise you may find yourself becoming over-sensitive. If this should occur, discontinue the meditation work for a week. If it persists, let us know. Meditation by this method is potent and has to be done carefully. It is not fool-proof.

Every day, at any hour convenient to yourself, but always at the same hour and if possible in the same place, repeat this meditation. Keep strictly to the method and exclusively to the subject set for the week. It is only by single-pointed team-work that results are obtained. A diffused benevolence never gets anywhere. Never attempt to deal with specific problems or to direct the course of affairs on the physical plane. Bring through spiritual force and leave it to that force to work its own way.

We shall be glad to hear from you once a month if you care to Communicate with us. Please mark your envelope "Meditation report".

> *8 October 1939 – Today, Adolf Hitler formally incorporated the Polish border areas into the German Reich.*

The first actual letter was dated October 8th 1939 and contains an important definition of the concepts of the Group Mind and the Group Soul.

LETTER 1
for October 8th 1939

The Fraternity of the Inner Light has for one of its rules the avoidance of all participation in politics, national or international, and these letters, sent to our members and friends whom the call of war has scattered, are no departure from that rule, for there are certain basic principles that transcend all partisanship; these are the prerogative of no party nor any nation, but are shared by all things living, because they are the laws of evolving life.

In the light of these spiritual principles we can guide our lives with steadfastness and certainty through all crises, and may know a sense of inner peace and security that cannot be shaken by any circumstances, not even death itself. And more than this, we can learn how best to bring such gifts as we have to give the common weal, for though there is no lack of good will and sacrifice, efficiency is not so common. Whatever we may be doing – active service, civil defence or our daily tasks, we should remember that it is a part of the One Life.

In times of universal stress, such as the present, we find ourselves sensitised to things of which we are normally unaware, or of which, though we may know in theory, we have had no personal experience. Among these is the Group-soul of the race. Who has not felt a sense of participation in this larger being, a total inability to insulate ourselves from it, however we might try? We realise with inescapable clearness that we are parts of a larger whole and that none can live unto himself.

We learn from actual experience the meaning of the words "We are all members one of another".

But in addition to the Group-soul, there is also the Group-mind, and we must distinguish between them in theory, though in practice they are inseparable. The Group-soul is to a race what the subconscious mind is to an individual; it contains the cumulative experience of the past. It acts as counterpoise against all shifts of the wind of changing circumstance so that, instead of being blown hither and thither, the trend of the crowd mind will be steadfast and predictable.

But the Group-soul of a nation is much more than a centre of stability; it is a source of inexhaustible dynamic energy, and we, as individuals, draw on it. We do this unconsciously in any case, but we can also do it consciously and deliberately and for specific purposes. The Group-mind, on the other hand, is comparatively superficial, shifting and veering with the surface currents and the winds of circumstance. It can be compared to the surface of consciousness of an individual. But though it is superficial in itself, it rests on the solid foundation of the Group-soul. Nevertheless, being unstable and easily influenced, it can be swayed by propaganda, by rumour, by personal feelings and the interests of individuals and groups, and it can, as it were, become detached from its solid base over considerable areas, rising up like bubbles on the surface of a boiling liquid. It is for us who understand the nature of the invisible realities and have trained ourselves in their use, to bring all our force to bear to hold the race life firmly together as a unified whole, welded to a spiritual basis like a house built upon a rock that cannot be moved.

15 October 1939 – Compulsory national service is introduced in Finland.

The second letter gave an example of one way in which occult meditation can work upon the Group Mind. The meditation work for the week given at the end of this letter was "Making contact with the spiritual influences ruling our race, using for this purpose the symbol of the Rose upon the Cross."

LETTER 2
for October 15th 1939

We have now made a start on the work we have set out to do – the opening of a channel whereby spiritual influences can contact the Group-mind of the race. We believe that there is a cosmic plan being worked out, of which the present conditions form a phase, and that we can consciously co-operate with the working of that plan. In confirmation of this belief I would like to draw attention to two things that have occurred. Either of these, of course, might be coincidence, but it is unlikely that they both would be.

Some eight weeks ago we decided to call together a group of our members and friends to form the nucleus of a meditation circle, and the date chosen for the first meeting was Sunday, October 1st. This date was chosen for psychic reasons as being the one on which the forces with which we proposed to co-operate would commence to flow. It is interesting to note that the same day was subsequently selected by the religious denominations of this country as a national day of prayer and intercession. May we not conclude from this that there is a current of spiritual force that moves in a definite manner, that there is something purposive and predictable in its workings, and that we are in touch with it?

Secondly, at the meeting held at 11 o'clock on Sunday morning Oct. 1st, in our Sanctuary at 3, Queensborough Terrace, the address and meditation instruction were based on the opening communication of the series, which were already stencilled and ready to be sent out on the appointed day. The members and friends there assembled meditated with a view to getting in touch with the Group-mind of the race in order that these teachings should be given to it through the invisible psychic channels that from time immemorial initiates have made use of in order to direct the Group-mind of the nation that they serve. Those who were assembled at that first meeting can bear witness to the fact that they were told that the ideas which were being used for the group meditations would inoculate the Group-mind of the race and would shortly be expressed in influential quarters that would ensure them a hearing, and that this was the way the Adepts, whose Group-mind forms the higher self of the race, have always worked.

At 8 p.m. on Monday evening, some thirty-six hours later, the address and meditation then given were repeated almost verbatim by the Archbishop of York broadcasting to the nation. Is this again a coincidence, or is it a further confirmation of the existence of spiritual influences at work on the Inner Planes?

I draw attention to these things not because I wish to boast, than which I dislike nothing more, but because of the confirmation they give of the occult teaching concerning the invisible governance of the world.

22 October 1939 – In a radio broadcast from Berlin, Josef Goebbels, Germany's minister of propaganda, calls Winston Churchill a liar.

In the third letter Dion Fortune was able to report some initial success.

LETTER 3
for October 22nd 1939

The work of building a channel of communication between the physical plane and the Inner Planes goes well. The results obtained in the group meditation on Sundays are proving very interesting and surprisingly good. To open the doors to all comers, as we have done, and out of those who enter, to form a meditation group for advanced work, is a very bold experiment indeed. It is one, in fact, that I would never have ventured upon had I not received express instruction concerning the withdrawing of the Veil. For many years I have protested against occult secrecy, though observing my oaths in the matter. Circumstances are such that I now have, within reasonable limits, a free hand. Traditional experience must necessarily be a guide, but it should not be a gaoler, especially when a new epoch inaugurates new conditions. At any rate, whatever may be the opinion of my fellow initiates upon my policy, the results appear to justify it.

29 October 1939 – In London this week, the government is given a white paper that exposes Nazi persecution of Jews and dissidents, and reveals the existence of concentration camps.

Results to justify Dion Fortune's "open door" policy were not slow in coming, as she describes in the fourth letter, which we quote in full.

LETTER 4
for October 29th 1939

The work of the group that meets on Sundays in the Sanctuary at 3, Queensborough Terrace, forms the focusing point of the meditation work that is done in response to these letters; not that it is impossible for people to make their own contacts individually, for this can always be done by those who know how, but because the meditation technique that we employ makes it possible for people who have not had any esoteric training to co-operate in the work. These will find it an interesting experience to observe the difference between individual work and organised group work.

The work of the group, like the work of each meditation period, goes in regular stages, systematically building up an organic structure on the Inner Planes. In this, the group meeting in the Sanctuary form the vanguard; where they have gone, the rest can follow without difficulty. Hitherto, we have been practising the technique of group symbol-making, which is exactly the same as that laid down for individuals in the Meditation Instructions issued with the first of these letters, save that a description of the symbols to be visualised is given by the leader of the meditation group, and the rest have to build them up as pictures in their imagination.

From the first we have had the interesting experience of the symbols "coming alive", thus indicating that they were "contacted" on the Inner Planes. The process is like building a bridge from both sides, those working on the Inner Planes building the thought-forms downward from the higher levels while we build upward from the earthly plane. Last Sunday we reached a point when it was no longer necessary to use the imagination to build the symbols, as these had now taken on definite astral forms and appeared and maintained themselves of their own accord. The reality of the astral forms was indicated by the fact that one member of the group, owing to association of ideas already established in connection with the symbols, got switched on to another line as a train is switched by the points, and found herself in the Sanctuary at Glastonbury in her vision, instead of at 3, Q.T.; and despite all her efforts, had to stay there till the meditation ended. This clearly shows that there is something much more in the meditation work than the use of imagination.

The work in the Sanctuary always starts with the symbol appointed from the group as a whole, and from this it develops like a growing plant throwing up a shoot, and from this shoot forms the basis of the work that is set out for the next week's task.

Starting from the symbol of the Rose upon the Cross, we immediately found it surrounded by golden light of great brilliance, while the Rose itself was outlined in what is called the Diamond Light, which indicates a very high grade of power indeed. It was then perceived that the golden light and the Cross were formulated inside a cavern. This told us where we were working.

This cavern is known to the initiates as the cavern beneath Mount Abiegnus, the Hill of Vision, of which the earthly symbol is Glastonbury Tor. It was at this point that the member of the Group who "missed the turning" found herself in the Sanctuary at Glastonbury, though the significance of the vision had not then been explained. It is also interesting to note that the Sanctuary in the garden of Chalice Orchard stands at the same height above sea level as the brick conduit through which water reaches the reservoir from the centre of the Tor, where a chamber must exist, though it has never been explored.

In the light that filled the cavern, five figures were discerned. These were not actual presences, but shadows thrown from a higher plane by the Masters with whom we shall be working; in due course they will formulate into the actual Presences.

Since writing the above words, the Sunday meeting has taken place, and as expected, the Presences formulated and the work of co-operation began. As will be remembered, the work undertaken was to bring to the race mind a realisation of the support afforded it by cosmic law. As we contacted the race mind, a tremendous sense of weight and resistance came down on the group as the gears engaged and the real work began – for hitherto we have been making our tools – and those sitting in the group had their first experience of what resisting astral forces can feel like. Then, as the concept of cosmic law was formulated, the weight lifted and we had a very remarkable sense of power and momentum. It was a fairly rough trip for inexperienced workers, but everyone came through well.

It is interesting to note that the ideas and ideals which we are trying to transmit to the mind of the race have once again been voiced in high places; those who heard the broadcast speech of Mr Hore-Belisha, Minister for War, could not fail to have been struck by the viewpoint and attitude expressed. In a letter that one of our members received from a highly placed German friend in America, the same note was struck. All these incidents may, of course, be coincidental, but the law of probability is against it.

We have now reached the point when the astral meeting place has been established, and in future those who join with us in the meditation exercises should visualise the Rose Cross as standing in the cave under the Hill of Vision, for this is now the meeting place. They should look for the figures of the Masters formulating in the golden light, and ought to have no difficulty in seeing at least the shadows.

> *5 November 1939 – In Moscow, Molotov blames the war on capitalist forces and says Russia's aim is peace.*

The work was consolidated during the following week, as the fifth letter indicates. Dion Fortune draws a firm line, in answer to a French correspondent, between positive and negative ways of working with the inner powers, and makes a forthright statement upon the question of pacifism.

LETTER 5
for November 5th 1939

Our work has now been proceeding for a month, and we are hoping to hear from those co-operating with us concerning the experiences they have received in the course of it. We have again an interesting experience to recount – in a speech made during the course of last week, the Pope gave expression to the ideals for which we are working, and, in addition, especially stressed the concept of spiritual law over-ruling all things, which it will be remembered was our meditation subject for last week. Far be it from us to suggest anything so foolish as that we are responsible for the Pope's speech, but we do claim that the incidents we have recorded from week to week are strong evidence in support of our contention that there is an active centre of spiritual influence on the Inner Planes that is "broadcasting" telepathically certain spiritual ideals.

The work of formulating the astral contacts is now completed. The Cross and the Cave built up of their own accord in the meditation performed in the Sanctuary on Sunday last. Until further notice the formulation of the Rose Cross and the Cave and the presence of the Masters in the light that shines upon the Cross should be performed at each meditation. At the last group meditation we perceived seven figures in the light, robed in the symbolic colours of the Rays, which are the colours of the spectrum. This indicates that we have now got our full range of contacts. We also perceived a great crowd of dark figures in the background, touched with light here and there. These represent those in the rank and file of the nation who are beginning to pick up telepathically the messages we are sending out. It is to be expected that the numbers of those participating in our work will soon be increasing.

The gold light changed into the Diamond Light as the meditation built up, and when we made contact with the group mind of the race we did not again feel the sense of stress and strain of the previous week, but instead a very wonderful sense of the steadfastness and the peace that comes from strength; there came a clear realisation that we do not have to lift the burden in our own strength, but to stand like an engineer with his hand on the lever that sets the machinery in motion. We have simply to pull the lever, and the Machinery of the Universe does the rest. Our work is to formulate and re-formulate day by day the mental link between the spiritual influences and the group mind of the race. This we do by means of our meditation work, and as we do it, we can, if we are at all sensitive, feel the power come through. The building of the images in the imagination is a purely mechanical act, like turning the starting-handle of a car; we use the reactions of our minds as indicators by means of which we read off what is happening on the Inner Planes and how the work is going. A little practice should enable all of you to do this with a considerable degree of accuracy.

We cannot do better than to continue on our work of realising the all powerful nature of spiritual law, in addition to the special meditation for each week. I received a letter from a French correspondent last week, urging that we should use our knowledge and power to make personal attacks on the leaders of the German nation in order to confuse their minds and even destroy their lives; but this would be quite the wrong way to work. Nothing and nobody is altogether evil, therefore it is never justifiable to try and destroy any person or thing by direct action, but only to open a channel whereby spiritual forces are brought to bear upon the problem. This is the meaning of Our Lord's command to leave the wheat and tares to grow together till the harvest. Hate is an evil thing in itself, whatever its provocation, and to call it righteous indignation does little to improve it.

Our work is a work of healing, and no hate must come of it. We look to see a regenerated Germany rise up in strength and greatness as well as goodwill and peace. On this great earth of ours there is room for all if they will only co-operate. All the time that we are working for a successful issue of the war, we must look forward to a happy peace of constructive comradeship. This thought should conclude every meditation. By an act of God's mercy, which we needed much more than we deserved it, we are being given a second chance to rebuild civilisation, a chance that was thrown away at Versailles and in the subsequent intrigues and inanities of Geneva. To achieve this peace there must be strength and integrity in the souls of the nations; there must be willingness to sacrifice individual national interests for the good of the whole, the strong remembering that they are in a better position to make sacrifices than the weak; but there must also be a readiness to unsheath and use the sword of justice when it is needed. It was this unwise reluctance to do this that led to the present war. Pacifism is too one-sided to be workable in an imperfect world, and has too often been made use of as a means of escape from hard reality. It is not well to pass by on the other side when thieves are beating honest men. This is no part of Christianity as I understand it.

12 November 1939 – King Leopold of Belgium and Queen Wilhelmina of the Netherlands offer to help in seeking "the elements of an agreement" before war begins in western Europe.

By the following week the pattern of symbols built up becomes a regular framework for future work, and Dion Fortune explains how it is that meditation work of this kind is important.

LETTER 6
for November 12th 1939

The formulation of the symbols and the building of the astral temple has been accomplished, so it is no longer necessary to give so much of our limited space to this side of the work. Our members and friends should continue week by week to use the formula of the Rose Cross, the Cave, and the seven Figures that come in the light. These will become more and more real to them week by week, and they will find developments arising out of them which we shall be interested to hear about in the monthly reports …

When we open our consciousnesses to spiritual forces by meditating thereon, we become channels for these forces, and when we do it in group formation, a very wide channel is opened and the forces come through with great power, far greater than the collective force of those forming the channel. Realising clearly the nature of evil, but not dwelling on it in meditation lest we accidentally contact it and expose ourselves to its disintegrating influence, let us work steadily day by day at bringing through the neutralising spiritual forces that shall hold it in abeyance and gradually neutralise it as an alkali neutralises an acid.

....
: *19 November 1939 – In Warsaw, barricades are being erected around the* :
: *Jewish ghetto.* :
....

In the seventh letter Dion Fortune outlines the theoretical basis for the formulation of astral imagery. Also detailed and very practical instruction on how to contact high spiritual forces and bring them through the astral channels.

LETTER 7
for November 19th 1939

Our work has now advanced so far that we have got a clear and well formulated astral image with which to operate. These thought-forms are the basis of all occult work; they are not 'real' in the sense that material objects or spiritual beings are real, being self-existent – for they are what initiates call "the creations of the created" – but they nevertheless have a very definite existence on the Inner Planes. They are used as a means of attracting and focusing forces, and to visualise them in the imagination is exactly like dialling a number on the telephone. Their use gives a power and clarity to meditation work that is never attained when purely abstract and mystical methods are used. Nevertheless, they are only a means to an end; and although we should fully realise their uses and value, we must never be superstitious over them. What the human mind has made, the human mind can unmake, and we could, if we wished, disperse them just as easily as we have made them. Unless they are dispersed by the proper means, however, they persist on the Inner Planes indefinitely, and can be revivified by anyone who has the necessary knowledge.

Mind-power, used in this way, is very potent, and it is therefore very necessary to be sure we are using it rightly. This is a very serious responsibility, so serious that no erring human being ought ever to take it upon themselves; therefore we never outline the form that the practical results should take on the physical plane, but always work in terms of ideals and spiritual principles and let the forces for which we build the channels express themselves according to their own nature. It may be asked how it is, since the methods outlined are so potent, that we have dared to reveal them openly. We dare to do this because we are acting under instruction, and the forces with which we are operating are under control from the Inner Planes. Any abuse of the forces would quickly be detected and dealt with, though not by us.

In order to work in terms of spiritual principles, we must realise them clearly and understand their nature. Just as the first month of our work was spent in building up the astral forms with which we intend to work, so we must now begin to bring through the spiritual forces that shall use them as channels. In order to do this, we must begin at the beginning of all things and picture the worlds coming into being. This may seem very remote from the pressing problems of the day, but its effects will quickly be realised if the attempt is made. People are already beginning to report that the work is having a marked effect on their health and nervous poise; the effect of this exercise will be found even more marked.

Being seated in your meditation posture, formulate the Cave, and then, instead of visualising the coming of the Presences, feel yourself to be seated alone there, in meditation. You will, in fact, do your meditation alone in the cave during the week, though on Sunday we shall all assemble as usual.

Picture to yourself the state of unmanifested existence on the eve of the dawn of a Cosmic Day. Picture it as a great ocean of indigo blue darkness, like the sky on a moonless night. Do not picture it as black, because that neutralises all activity. Then imagine a shaft of dim light, like a searchlight, penetrate the darkness and begin to swing with a circling motion.

Visualise currents of light being set up by this circular motion; see them grow brighter and brighter and take on colours. Repeat to yourself as a litany or mantram the words: "The Rings and the Rays swing into being."

Imagine yourself standing poised on the globe of Earth with arms lifted in invocation as it swings in its orbit through space. There is a famous picture by G.F. Watts that can serve as a model, reproductions of which can be obtained for a few pence. The coloured plates in astronomy books also help the realisation. Out of all these, build up a mental picture of the beginnings of evolution and imagine yourself as part of it, swinging through space with the movement of the cosmic tides. Remember that you actually were part of it, though in an unevolved state, and that the experiences then undergone remain deep in your subconscious memory, and that they will be aroused by the reconstructing of the picture images. The result of this work will be to put you in touch with primordial causation.

Having obtained a clear mental picture by means of the foregoing exercise, remind yourself that these forces still operate on the highest levels of the Inner Planes, and it is their perfect rhythm and balance which determines that harmony of all the levels of manifestation, like the flywheel of a vast machine. Think of this enormous swirl and rhythm as carrying with it, like leaves on a stream, the nations and their affairs, so that, however much they may swirl in eddies among themselves, the main current is all the time bearing them away to the Great Ocean of Being.

The purpose of this exercise is to prepare a basis for the realisation that all things are parts of a single Whole, which is the Being of God. It is the first stage in the work, and the foundation must be well and thoroughly laid by clear realisation before the next stage can be commenced, but at the same time the relation of the part to the whole must be borne in mind.

> *28 November 1939 – In London the go-ahead is given for the seizure of German goods on the high seas.*

Much of the teaching in the previous letter is based upon the principles in Dion Fortune's work *The Cosmic Doctrine,* mediumistically received at the commencement of her founding the Community of the Inner Light in 1923-4. This was used as an advanced study text for members of the Society, although not publicly published until after the war. This grounding of the work in hand with abstract spiritual principles is put into effect with the meditation subject for this period: "The realisation of the Rings and the Rays swinging into being."

In her eighth letter she recapitulates the method and rationale of occult working and its relation to mysticism. And brings the focus of attention down from the root principles of the equilibrium of the cosmos as figured in the Rings and the Rays to specific contact with the unseen helpers behind the group and the nation, the work for the week being "to realise the comradeship of the Elder Brethren."

LETTER 8
for November 28th 1939

It is this combination of the mental with the spiritual, or the spiritual with the mental, according to the degree of knowledge possessed by those who do it, that constitutes the difference between occultism and mysticism. We are engaged on the mental aspect of the work; those who come to us in the light are engaged on the spiritual aspect of it; neither would be effectual without the other but together we can almost literally move mountains. It is in this manner that over and over again the souls of nations have been influenced by invisible guidance. What we are doing is nothing new in the history of the Mystery Tradition, but it has never before been explicitly stated save to those who have taken the Oath of the Mysteries; that it can be revealed in these letters is due to the fact that a new epoch has commenced.

We are not so foolish or fantastic as to claim that our work as a meditation group is controlling the fate of nations; but we do claim, and not without evidence in support of the claim, that we are sharing in activities which are exercising a definite influence in world affairs. Those who have co-operated with us thus far cannot fail to be aware that something beyond the human mind is at work. Now comes the time when we begin to put our faith to the test.

The feeling that we are not isolated individuals but part of a disciplined army, gives us a sense of confidence in the effectiveness of what we are doing, which is half the battle in Inner Plane working. We especially need this week to gain a realisation of the work that is being done by those whom we call the Elder Brethren; those who come to us in the light, and of whom we have already, in varying degrees, had experience. Their presence should become increasingly real and tangible to us.

They are indeed real personalities and their presence is an actual fact, even though the form under which we perceive them is an image in the imagination. It corresponds to reality, and is used to form the psychic link. Its use will be found to be effectual. To those who have not yet achieved a realisation, or who have not got as clear a realisation as they could wish, I would say: Act 'as if' what I state were true; take it as a working hypothesis and give it the benefit of the doubt, and you will soon feel the 'sense of reality' that comes when those on the Inner Planes get in touch. It is our faith that enables them to get in touch with us in the first place, but once the contact is made, faith soon hardens with the certainty of experience.

3 December 1939 – This week conscription is extended to include all men of 19 to 41 years of age.

A certain amount of stress and unbalanced force was beginning to be felt by many of those engaged in the work, and in the ninth letter Dion Fortune describes how to cope with this kind of problem, which occurs whenever powerful contacts are being effectively made.

In this same letter she goes on to make an interesting observation about mediumship and its place in the armamentarium of occult techniques. Much of her own best work was obtained by this means and although it is a modus operandi that is easily abused, she felt strongly that there was a place for it, properly used in the context of an occult group. Part of this was as a kind of power contact, at quarterly meetings of the group when most members were present, even the most junior, when a "trance address" would be made. Apart from the verbal content of the communication on these occasions she regarded them as an important means of inner contact for those not yet capable of making their own conscious inner contacts very readily. Nonetheless, this did not obscure the important point that no-one should be reliant on another's mediumship, the idea being to "be one's own medium", and in these unusual times the opportunity for this was great.

LETTER 9
for December 3rd 1939

Because we are, by reason of the work we are doing in this group, in close touch with the soul of the race, we shall be able to experience its stresses and to find them reflected in our affairs, stirring into activity whatever latent sources of trouble may be lying dormant. These personal problems can be dealt with in meditation in just the same way as the work for the nation has been done. It will be found a great help, in this respect, to visualise the presence of the Master with whom one feels the greatest affinity, and to conduct with him an imaginary conversation in which we tell our troubles and imagine the answer being given to us. These imaginary conversations, colloquies, as they are called by mystics, enable us to get in touch with the Masters, and even if we are not sufficiently developed psychically to hear the reply, we get an extraordinary sense of peace and support from the contact. If we perform this meditation practice last thing at night, we will frequently find that when we awake in the morning the situation has clarified, for that which was heard by the subconscious mind only, has worked through into consciousness during sleep, so that although we may not hear directly the voice of the Master, we get the message quite clearly.

This method or working is well understood by mystics as well as occultists, and it will be seen that in entirely eliminates the necessity to employ a medium. The initiates have always maintained that one should be one's own medium, and this is how it is done.

Because we are getting in touch so closely with the group mind of the race, we shall find ourselves increasingly liable as individuals to be affected by its ups and downs; but as fellow workers with the Elder Brethren we have the right to ask for help and advice if we feel we need them. I would urge all our friends and fellow workers to avail themselves of this opportunity to establish contacts with the Masters for it does not often happen that the veil is as thin as it is at the moment. The power and tangibility of the response that comes through will astonish those who are new to this method of working.

We are fully entitled to help and protection in any difficulties or stresses we are exposed to through our participation in the Masters' work, and this help is unfailingly forthcoming if it is invoked. I would again urge my readers to take advantage of what may be a unique opportunity of obtaining very valuable first hand experience of the invisible realities.

In spite of attacks made on mediumship by Mme. Blavatsky and others of her school, initiates of the Western Tradition do not decry its use under the right conditions; it is indiscriminate use that they deplore. Mediumship is made use of in the occult schools in the same way as an amplifier is made use of in a lecture hall – it is employed when a Master wants to speak to a number of people at the same time. The initiate, however, is always taught to be very careful not to come to depend on such 'broadcasting' to the neglect of his own development. A good psychic can often pick up the message that is coming through a medium a sentence or two ahead of the spoken word – that is to say, if the message is a genuine one. The value of a message obtained through mediumship as used by initiates does not depend only on what is said, which may be no more than a few words of blessing, but upon the very powerful psychic atmosphere that is generated by the Master who is projecting the message. All these things are part of the training and work of the Mysteries, so it is necessary that those who participate in this work should have an understanding of this.

28 January 1940 – This week in Spain, the Council of Ministers outlaws Freemasonry. In Poland, Jews are forbidden to travel by train.

The letters that follow contain general theoretical points that are readily accessible in published work, in response to various questions that had apparently been put to Dion Fortune by less experienced participants in this series of workings.

When the fifteenth letter was issued, the inner tide that runs between the Winter Solstice and the Vernal Equinox was in full spate. The meditation work for the week had been "To invoke the purifying Tides of Destruction upon whatever is obsolete, selfish and inefficient in our country." And Dion Fortune duly reports the results.

Furthermore, towards the end of this letter we have a new development in the work, in the invocation of angelic protectors for the country.

LETTER 15
for January 28th 1940

On Sunday, in the Sanctuary, we meditated on the Tides of Destruction, fearlessly invoking their purifying force. This is a bold thing to do at any time, and particularly so when working with an untrained group, but the results entirely justified the experiment. The outline of the astral images was peculiarly steady and solid, and the power came down in the symbolic form of a great jet of steel-grey water behind which, in the centre of the circle, appeared the red-robed Master of the Ray of Geburah. There was a tremendous sense of strength under control, of steadiness, of a complete grip on the forces that were being brought through. At the end of the meditation, when the Banishing Pentagrams had returned all to normal, there was a profound sense of peace and protection that was remarked on by all present …

We must hold firmly before the soul of the race a bracing, astringent ideal, not relaxing our watch or laying down our weapons till the word is given. A premature and unsound peace would be disastrous. Our increasing confidence lays us open to subtle influencing, against which we must guard.

In order to guard against any such subtle influencing, let us meditate upon angelic Presences, red-robed and armed, patrolling the length and breadth of our land. Visualise a map of Great Britain, and picture these great Presences moving as a vast shadowy form along the coasts, and backwards and forwards from north to south and east to west, keeping watch and ward so that nothing alien can move unobserved.

4 February 1940 – HMS Sphinx, a mine-sweeper, sinks after being bombed by German planes.

The importance of the angelic work is immediately taken up in the letter following, together with an interesting note about the preparatory work for these letters. Finland, it might be noted, according to teaching by Rudolf Steiner and his followers on the folk angels of the nations, has a special place in Europe as custodian of very pure and early spiritual contacts, partly revealed in their folk epic, *The Kalevala*.

LETTER 16
for February 4th 1940

The work of the formulation of the Angelic Presences is so valuable that it might well be continued, in addition to the usual weekly meditations, 'for the duration'. It is interesting to note that at the time this meditation instruction was being prepared, such Presences were reported in the papers as having been seen in Finland.

Now these letters are prepared after 'skrying' the astral conditions prevailing in this country and in Germany, in addition to which, definite instructions are received from the Elder Brethren from time to time, but not every week. It was in obedience to such special instructions that the meditation work on the Angelic Presences was sent out. The fact that such Presences were perceived at the same time in Finland seems to show that similar instructions were received there. It is obvious, therefore, that they are 'receiving' on the same psychic wave-length that we are, and is probable that the future will see a close union between Finland and this country.

11 February 1940 – Paper supplies are cut by 40% as rationing is introduced. In Birmingham, five IRA bombs explode.

The seventeenth letter sees the beginning of a developing symbol complex that is to play an important role in the work to come. One of the hallmarks of truly contacted occult work is the way that symbol systems will build organically and reveal a sequence of development when later reviewed analytically. Starting as a simple triangle of coloured light, Dion Fortune gives some basic elucidation by reference to the Tree of Life.

LETTER 17
for February 11th 1940

During the meditation in the Sanctuary last Sunday, a symbol of great interest and importance formulated in the course of the vision of the cave. Those who come to meet with us in the Light had taken up their usual position at the foot of the Cross, forming with us a circle, and the influences of the incoming life-tide were invoked under the symbol of down-pouring light. The light appeared at first as the dim grey dawn-light; this soon became flecked with many colours like a fire opal. Then it clarified into three definite Rays, forming the three angles of a triangle with the white light of the Spirit pouring down within it.

These three Rays were the Red, the Blue and the Purple, and there is an important significance in the colour symbolism, especially as the vision formulated spontaneously, and the significance of the symbolism was not realised immediately. The Red Ray is the dynamic, destructive Ray of Mars, issuing from the Sephirah Geburah, with which we have been working recently. Those who are familiar with the Tree of Life will remember that Geburah, or severity, stands opposite Gedulah (Chesed), mercy, from which issues the Blue Ray of Jupiter, and that these two are represented in symbolism as the two kings. The one, Geburah, robed in red, is armed and mailed, riding in a chariot, the sword of justice in his hand. The other, Gedulah, robed in blue, sits upon a throne, the sceptre of wisdom in his hand, and he is the king in time of peace, just as the Lord of Geburah is the king in time of war. The one represents the dynamic forces of a nation, military and judicial – for we get the same scarlet in the robes of the judges as in the soldier's uniform; the other represents the organising, socialising, civic forces of national life, the royal blue of the king as law-giver and administrator, shepherding his people …

The Master Jesus is said to be the Lord of the Purple Ray. Those who are familiar with the Tree of Life will remember that Tiphareth is the Christ Centre where all forces are brought into equilibrium; but in Yesod, whose colour is purple, the personality aspect of the Christ force is reflected downwards into manifestation. Moreover, Yesod is called the Receptacle of Forces and its proper symbol is the Cup, or Graal, which is the antithesis in equilibrium of the Sword, Excalibur. When the time comes for reconstruction, we shall have occasion to work with these forces and the Excalibur forces in balanced equilibrium, and the Cup and the Sword and Sceptre make a wonderful symbol of balanced and functional force. This triple-rayed triangle is unquestionably a very important symbol for us, and it should be in future formulated in meditations in a horizontal position above the Rose Cross in the Cave.

18 February 1940 - The Polish air force is allowed to reform on French soil. In Munich, Hitler says, "We cannot be defeated either economically or militarily ..."

The group had been set to concentrate upon the Triangle described in the previous letter, and the following, eighteenth, letter is full of interesting technical detail as the basic geometrical imagery crystallises into three key symbols – of rod, sword and cup.

LETTER 18
for February 18th 1940

When we built up the symbol of the three Rays of the Triangle in our group meditation on Sunday, certain very striking and illuminating things occurred – things, that is to say, that have much significance when there is the knowledge to interpret them.

At the commencement the meditation lacked power. Now to the experienced worker an operation that goes wrong is just as instructive as one that goes right, in fact even more so. We had to ask ourselves why it was that a symbol that had been full of power the previous week should lack power seven days later. The answer was not far to seek in the light of experience. The previous week the vision of the three Rays had not been built up by the action of either leader or group, but had appeared spontaneously; what was described had not been formulated but was being reported as it took form of its own undirected accord; it must, therefore, have been projected down the planes by Those with whom we are co-operating, and therefore, being ensouled with spiritual force, possessed a singular vividness. When we, however, following the usual technique, proceeded to build up the form in our imaginations, it lacked this ensouling force, and therefore appeared dim and dead, and there was no power in the room.

But experience was again our guide, and we persevered with the uphill task, and presently power began to come in. It did not come in the shape of a brightening of the Rays into the vividness with which we had seen them the previous week, but shadowy forms began to appear where the Rays touched the plane of Earth. Immediately this occurred, power came through. From this experience a useful lesson is to be learnt – that mind-work without thought-forms is very little use.

These forms were not so much presences as simulacra; that is to say, one had no sense of personality in regard to them and they appeared like line drawings within the coloured Rays. It is not easy to say exactly what they were, but it is to be presumed that they were projected by the same entities who had previously projected the Rays. We may learn more about them later.

The form in the Red Ray was that of the mailed and armed King with a crown upon his helm – the traditional form of Geburah, save that in this instance he was not seated in his war chariot but mounted upon a charger, thus representing an exceedingly dynamic form of the energy of the fifth Sephirah. He appeared, however, to be turned partly away from us, so that we saw him from the side and rear. This signifies that the destructive force is not directed towards us, but is acting defensively by attacking. The form in the Blue Ray was the traditional one of the King seated on his throne. The form in the Purple Ray was that of the Master Jesus in his aspect as the Risen Christ, clad in a Seamless Robe.

Then, these pictures having formulated, for they were definitely pictures and not personalities, a symbol began to stand out clearly in connection with each of them. In the Red Ray it was the sword grasped in the hand of the mailed rider; in the Blue Ray, it was the sceptre held in the hand of the seated figure; in the Purple Ray, it was a cup carried by Our Lord – the Cup of the Graal.

Those who have experience in these matters know that it is in this form that the higher communications are made. If what is to be communicated comes from a plane beyond human consciousness, words cannot be used as a means of communication, a symbol appears, and if we meditate upon it, realisation gradually dawns; it also acts as a link or means of communication with Those who sent it, for meditating thus is exactly like dialling a number on the telephone – it puts us in touch with that which the symbol represents. It is, in fact, exactly as if someone were to give you his telephone number so that you could put through a call whenever you wanted to. Usually, in esoteric work, these key-calls are kept very secret, but as this one was given openly, it is evidently meant to be passed on openly, and I am therefore giving it so that all who wish to do so may use it. On the other hand, these key-calls can be made use of by persons who might wish to break up what we are doing. I think, however, that the entities at the other end of the line are very well able to take care of themselves; the forces with which we work are not innocuous, and we may as well face the fact that they can blast as well as bless. It would not be well to call up that number in the wrong spirit.

It now remains for us to find out the significance of the three symbols taken together, thus forming a glyph, which is a composite symbol. They represent a formula, the formula with which it may be presumed we are to work. Let us consider them individually. The sword of Geburah, the sphere of Mars, means the dynamic force destroying evil; it is Excalibur, the Sword of Chivalry. The sceptre is the Rod of Power whereby the Invisible Forces are ruled and directed; being in the hands of the seated King of the Sephirah Chesed or Gedulah, the sphere of the planet Jupiter, it means that the knowledge which directs these forces is to be applied to the governance of the race. The Cup is a symbol of many significances; it is associated with Isis as the Moon-cup, the symbol of womanhood, and with Christ as the Graal, the receptacle of spiritual influences; the receptive aspect, of course, links it also with womanhood. These three symbols, conjoined, represent a formula which it is our task to work with and work out.

25 February 1940 – American envoy, Sumner Welles, arrives in Rome to start talks for European peace.

In her nineteenth letter Dion Fortune gives some guidance on the significance of one of the three symbols – the Rod of Power – and goes on to make some astute observations, based on experience, of the nature and significance of esoteric work, even by a few dedicated and trained souls. She is also in no doubt about the occult powers being deliberately invoked by the forces of Hitler's Third Reich. As I have described in *The Magical World of the Inklings* (Skylight Press, 2010), the occult nature of these forces were also characterised in their true colours by C.S. Lewis' science fiction novel *That Hideous Strength*. In matter of fact terms described by Dion Fortune, we see the actuality of some of the behind the scenes activity in the war between these forces of darkness and light.

LETTER 19
for February 25th 1940

The symbol we will consider this week is that of the Figure seen in the Blue Ray – the King upon his throne with the sceptre, the Rod of Power in his hand. This symbolism belongs to the Sephirah Chesed, also called Gedulah or Mercy, in equilibrium with Geburah or Severity. It is the Sphere of Jupiter, as Geburah is the sphere of Mars, and represents Jupiter well aspected in all its benign majesty and dignity. It is the sign of the King in peace, directing and governing his people, and its distinguishing symbol is the sceptre. Now this sceptre is the Rod of Power and signifies occult knowledge directing the astral forces. This teaches us that the knowledge of the Secret Wisdom is going to play an important part in what has to be done for the winning of the war and the building of a stable peace. This may sound fantastic, but it is only necessary to read the unexpurgated edition of *Mein Kampf* to see that the Nazis are fully alive to this, and that the manipulation of the racial subconscious mind is one of the strongest cards they play. This card can only be trumped by a higher card of the same denomination – military force is ineffectual against it, and it is here that our specialised knowledge can be of very real use. I had not read *Mein Kampf* at the time when I started these meditations, but now that I have read it, I can see plainly to what end they are directed, and why it is urgently necessary that they should be carried on. It may be a very small handful of leaven that we are providing, but the nature of the spiritual force employed is such that it is capable of leavening the whole mass of racial subconsciousness and immunising it from Nazi poison.

Let us meditate this week upon the tremendous forces wielded by means of that Rod of Power. They are far greater than we realise at present. Esoteric tradition has always averred that certain work in connection with the spiritual advancement of mankind is carried out by small groups of trained and dedicated persons set here and there among the nations, working unknown and in secret, and there is no intrinsic reason why we should not be one of them. For many years prior to the war, the Fraternity of the Inner Light has so believed and taught. All that is necessary for this purpose is a nucleus of six or more sincerely dedicated persons gathered round one who has the necessary knowledge. If tradition is to be believed, we shall make a mistake if we underestimate the powers that are working through us. We may have little enough that is spectacular to show, but the work we set out to do is obviously getting done. Nor is it being done in any random manner, but step by step, in the precise order which we have been instructed to do it. It is only necessary to read over the whole series of meditation instructions in conjunction with a week by week record of the war to see the correlation. Bearing in mind that we were told at the commencement that this would be so, we can see that the traditional Rod of Power, the Diamond Sceptre, still exercises its invisible influence, and by the methods that have always been credited to it.

Still the war is being confined to the Inner Planes, and the amazing rise in the morale of the nation indicates the way in which the fight is going. A blitzkrieg today would have a very different effect on us to what it would have had last autumn. With every week that passes, the spiritual tide is rising, and an energy and confidence is showing itself to which this country has been a stranger many a long day. England has always had confidence in itself and distrusted its leadership – lions led by donkeys is the traditional axiom; but today it is beginning to feel that it has a leadership that it can trust.

3 March 1940 – Sumner Welles meets with Goering in Berlin who evades his inquiries about alleged cruelty to Polish Jews.

Practical teaching is continued in the twentieth letter, with the significant addition that the accompanying meditation changes from "The Rod of Power" to "The Use of the Rod of Power". A list of the meditation subjects that accompany the letters is given on page 175, and as Dion Fortune pointed out in her previous letter, their sequence is quite instructive.

LETTER 20
for March 3rd 1940

The Rod of Power, or Diamond Sceptre, is a concept well know to those who study the Secret Tradition. No doubt in the past it given symbolic form as a rod, possibly jewelled, but actually it i trained mind of the initiate.

In earlier letters we considered the ways in whi could be instilled telepathically into the group mind of a r meone who was a member of that race, and who therefore had access to its group mind, living them out in actual practice "with intention". It will be noted, however, that we have defined the Rod of Power as the trained mind of an initiate, not merely as the trained mind. An initiate, by virtue of his knowledge and training, is in touch with cosmic forces, and he makes himself a channel for their manifestation, his mind selecting and directing them. This is the real Diamond Sceptre.

For the use of this method a group of trained and dedicated people is needed. The training is in the traditional method of the Mysteries whereby control not only of the mind but also of the magnetic forces of the etheric double is obtained. The dedication is first to the One, Unity, the Godhead, source of all being and measure of all good; and secondly to one or another of the great mystical Orders that lie in the background of the different traditions. In our own case, the Order is indicated by the symbol we use to open our meditation and pick up our contacts, and the Tradition, it need hardly be said, is the Western. All the Orders are brethren, however, and all the Paths converge upon Unity, the difference between them being indicated by the word Tradition, which means that they have evolved under the influence of different types of culture.

All who care to take the work seriously can be of help in this task and participate in its experiences. They can all form facets of the Diamond Sceptre, helping with the transmission of the spiritual influences thus invoked. Once the link is made, the power is soon flowing spontaneously. Knowledge is needed to pick up the force and to direct it, and this knowledge is supplied by the leader of a group, but none who are sincerely dedicated to the love and service of man and God need feel that they are without value in the work. Naturally, the more knowledge and trained mind-power there is, the better, but devotion and deep spiritual feeling contribute to the work something for which knowledge alone is no substitute. Those who have the knowledge necessary for the work need the help of those who have the devotion for its carrying out. Therefore all who so desire can co-operate in a spirit of devotion, and those who are able to go further can have an opportunity to do so.

10 M... the Ki*40 – Meat rationing is introduced this week. Sumner Welles meets ...*eville Chamberlain in London to discuss peace proposals.

The twenty-first letter brings in the significance of the other two symbols, the sword and the cup, and Dion Fortune shows how all three interlink into a composite glyph that takes the work on from immediate defence to positive long term construction.

LETTER 21
for March 10th 1940

We are now engaged upon a phase of our work which is not merely defensive but constructive, and defensive because it is constructive. We are, in fact, working out the formula of the new aeon.

We have already worked upon the symbol of the Sceptre, or Rod of Power, and interpreted it as meaning the Secret Wisdom employed to guide the affairs of nations. But there are two other symbols in the glyph and we cannot understand any one of them in its full significance apart from its relationship to the other two.

These two are the Sword and the Cup made familiar to us in Arthurian Legend. Those who are instructed in the use of the symbolic method of meditation in conjunction with the diagram of the Tree of Life know that all symbols possess a fourfold significance attributed to the four planes of manifestation, and the Diamond Sceptre is no exception to this rule. Upon the highest plane it represents the power that comes to a man when he knows the will of God and places himself in alignment with it; upon the mental plane it represents the power that comes from a knowledge of the true nature of things; upon the astral plane it represents the magical skill that controls and directs the astral forces; upon the physical plane it represents the strength of the human will.

This fourfold interpretation applies equally to the other two symbols that complete the triangle of force. Neither of these, however, can be understood apart from the other, for they are a Pair of Opposites; each, taken separately, is a great half truth, and so misleading. They must therefore never be considered apart. This, of course, is true of any symbol, which must always be considered in relationship to its opposite if a full understanding is to be obtained of its significance, for all manifestation is dual, unity being Unmanifest.

The Sword and the Cup, on the physical plane, represent the positive and negative forces of the universe and can, according to the method of the Qabalah, be attributed to Chokmah and Binah. Upon the mental plane the Sword presents the scientific, critical, discerning intellect; the

Cup represents the imaginative, intuitive, artistic qualities of the mind. Upon the astral plane they represent the method of the occultist and the method of the psychic. Upon the physical plane they represent the masculine and feminine potencies, thus being the material reflections of Chokmah and Binah. Here we have a mass of symbolism that will afford food for meditation for many a long hour, gradually unfolding its significance as it is brooded over.

To sum up briefly, the glyph as a whole refers to spiritual power, directed by occult knowledge, operating through the positive and negative forces of the universe upon all four planes of manifestation.; we know that our work as a whole is concerned with the life of the nation; the glyph may therefore be taken as being a formula of regeneration for the race.

17 March 1940 – After talks in Italy with Mussolini, Sumner Welles ends US efforts to bring the war to an end and returns home.

The first six months of weekly letters is brought to a fine close with the twenty-second, which appears in the week of the Vernal Equinox of 1940. Here Dion Fortune spells out plainly the nature of the inner contacts that constitute the "greater mysteries" behind her work, the Rosicrucian Tradition. Furthermore, she lays down the line of the importance of the Arthurian legend for future work, with particular emphasis on the role of Merlin, seen as a coloniser from a higher and older civilisation. This work was indeed considerably developed in the years before her death, and most of this material I was permitted to incorporate into *The Secret Tradition in Arthurian Legend* (Aquarian Press, 1983), and as *The Arthurian Formula* (Thoth, 2006).

LETTER 22
for March 17th 1940

When the group that meets on a Sunday at 3, Q.T. meditated upon the direction in which the Diamond Sceptre points, certain things began to come clear. It is obvious that we are dealing with Arthurian symbolism in the Cup and the Sword, and it would seem to fit in well with the nature of the glyph if we take the Armed King on his battle charger in the Red Ray as King Arthur, and the Throned King in the Blue Ray as Merlin, for Merlin undoubtedly was the law giver to the Kingdom of Britain and his power was the power of the Secret Wisdom, as all legends attest. The work we are doing, as we already know, derives its primary contact from the Rosicrucian Tradition, but its expression in the outer world will evidently be through the Arthurian branch of that Tradition.

It may seem strange to speak of the Mysteries of the Graal as an aspect of the Rosicrucian Tradition, which they long ante-dated, but for practical purposes that is correct. The Western Esoteric Tradition, as the mystical knowledge of the Christian nations is collectively called, consists, as do all esoteric traditions, of the Greater and Lesser Mysteries. The Rosicrucian Tradition is the repository of the secret wisdom of the ancient Mystery religions, Neo-Platonism and alchemy. Those Lesser Mysteries of the Britons and the Kelts, which are known to us as the Arthurian Cycle of legends, derive according to both intrinsic and psychic evidence, from Ancient Mysteries.

A Lodge of the Lesser is always the pendant of a Greater Mystery Temple, and as the Rosicrucian Order is the lineal descendent and repository of the ancient Mystery Tradition, it is quite correct to speak of the Mysteries of the Graal as part of the Rosicrucian Tradition, for so they are at the present time, for the good and excellent reason that they cannot be worked apart from Rosicrucian knowledge. In the light of this explanation, it can be seen how our work has gradually unfolded like a flower growing from living roots, thus affording clear evidence of the truth of the claim that instructions for its carrying out are being received from the Inner Planes.

We know, therefore, that whatever form our work will subsequently take, it will be expressed in terms of Arthurian symbolism and rooted in the Arthurian Tradition. This affords us a further interesting piece of information, for the Arthurian Tradition is closely linked up with the Keltic Church, the primitive pre-Roman Christianity in these islands, brought hither direct from the Holy Land by Joseph of Arimathea, the Graal-bearer. This is to us a most important key, for our problem has been to maintain the Christian contacts while freeing ourselves from the misleading bondage of what Mme. Blavatsky so aptly termed Churchianity.

In the primitive Christianity of these islands we touch something very simple and pure and very close to Nature, for there were no disputes between the priests of the Sun and the priests of the Son when the inspiration of the Graal first came to these islands – the one merged naturally into the other.

Merlin was unquestionably a druid priest and tradition declares him to be an Atlantean, King Arthur was equally unquestionably, and apparently with Merlin's full agreement, a Christian knight. Consequently we have a tradition of Christian chivalry with the ancient teaching of the Graal. Here is indeed a rich field for our tilling.

From this source we can draw an inspiration that is native to these islands though not limited thereto, for the legends ramify all over Europe through the Quests of the various knights.

We may take it, then, that it is Merlin, the Ancient Wise One, who points with the sceptre the direction in which we are to go.

21 April 1940 – In Norway, Norwegian and British troops are forced out of Lillehammer by German forces.

There was a period of relative inactivity following the Vernal Equinox of 1940. There had been a pause in the regularity of the weekly meetings as a result of the Whitsun holidays, and as Dion Fortune pointed out in her twenty-third letter, it would take a week or two to build up to the previous momentum. The pause seems to have been salutary because, in the twenty-fifth letter, the atmosphere of serenity that pervades the group's headquarters, and that surrounds all who take part in the work, is commented upon. But at the same time loins are girded up for action in the formulation of an angelic patrol, not only around the immediate coasts of the British Isles, but extending far over the North Sea.

LETTER 25
for April 21st 1940

It will be noted that the earth of England is still immune from the forces of destruction. In this connection I would like to point out the significance of certain things. Firstly, our headquarters at 3, Q.T. is a centre of peace, so much so that it is only when we leave its atmosphere that we realise how profoundly peaceful and completely safe-guarded that atmosphere is. It must not be thought that we are selfishly indifferent to the fate of our own and other nations when I say that for us at 3, Q.T. the war might be non-existent so far as any mental strain is concerned.

This is as it should be; firstly, because if it were otherwise, we could not be a centre of radiation, and secondly because it proves that we are doing our work efficiently – physician, heal thyself! If we were unable to maintain an atmosphere of serenity in our own head-quarters, how could we hope to be a nucleus of stability for the group-soul of the nation? Moreover, we ourselves could not do the work that is required of us if we had not got an atmosphere of serenity to do it in.

And not only is there an atmosphere of stability and serenity at our head-quarters, but the meditation reports and letters of those who are working with us show that they, as individuals, find themselves stabilised and sharing in this serenity; they are in a remarkable degree individual nuclei of stability in a profoundly disturbed world.

This stability is in part due to the power of steady meditation to neutralise inco-ordinated vibrations; it is also no doubt due to our certainty of the outcome of the war, because the power of extended vision can see how things are going on the Inner Planes and deduce their outcome. This is not prophecy in the ordinary sense of the word; but just as a man on a high cliff can see a ship approaching the shore before it is visible to those at sea level, so, when we are able to perceive conditions on the planes of causation, we are able to announce the advent of events of which we have watched the causes.

It is no vain or unverifiable boasting to declare that we have succeeded in building a sphere of psychic protection over our own head-quarters, and that, using the same methods, those who are co-operating with us have built the same kind of psychic bell-jar over themselves.

It will also be noted that a similar kind of circuit of protection guards our shores. The life of these islands goes on in peace, for the tide of war is held back at high water-mark; thus it has been for the first vital six months of the war, when our defences were in the making; is there any reason to doubt that it will continue to be so now that our physical preparations are completed and ready for all eventualities? Germany, we know, had nothing to add to the readiness of her air force when war broke out.

Meanwhile, with the war entering upon its active phase, we must continue to keep watch and ward of the astral ways, and we should again concentrate upon the angelic patrol of our coasts. But we might also try to advance our boundaries, and those who have a taste for psychic adventure might get a map, or mark out on a map, the long line of the mine-fields that run from the far north down the coast of Norway, divide into two at the passage to the Baltic, and wall off both eastern and western sea-boards of Germany. It may quite well be that Germany has received her last seaborne imports and we have heard the last of commerce raiders.

Such a patrol will be stormy work, and only those with steady nerves should attempt it. In order to do it, a mental picture of the map of Europe in that area should be combined with a mental picture of the rocky shores or sandy coasts of the region patrolled. The experiment should first be made of patrolling the North Sea coastline, and only when it is proved possible to do this steadily and clearly should the attempt be made to carry the patrol through the narrow waters into the Baltic.

> *28 April 1940 – This week, Germany officially declares war on Norway. Within three days the Allies are forced to evacuate 4000 men. Their equipment has to be left behind.*

Immediately following upon the extension of their work, an added dimension is found in the symbolic images that they had been formulating. In a sense this is an interesting development in the light of Dion Fortune's latter novels, and might well be seen as a higher aspect of the Isis contacts.

LETTER 26
for April 28th 1940

A very interesting development of our work took place on Sunday April 21st during the meeting in the Sanctuary at 3, Q.T. We built the Cross, the Cavern and the Triangle as usual, and were contemplating the Triangle with the three Figures in the Rays, when it was seen that the third Figure had, for the first time, become the focus of the meditation.

It will be remembered that the Red and the Blue Rays were taken respectively as Geburah and Chesed and the Purple Ray as Yesod, and that the mounted Figure in the Red Ray, bearing the Sword, was taken to be King Arthur, and the seated Figure in the Blue Ray, holding the Sceptre, was taken to be Merlin; the third Figure, standing in the Purple Ray and holding the Cup, was taken to be the Master Jesus.

Now this attribution presented certain difficulties, for the Master Jesus, being on an altogether different plane to King Arthur and Merlin, formed an unbalanced triangle unless He were taken as emanating the other two, and as the point of contemplation is from Malkuth, looking towards Yesod, it will be seen that this attribution presented difficulties which our workers may have discovered for themselves. Nevertheless, we had to take what we were given and do the best we could with it, waiting for its significance to unfold.

In the meeting in the Sanctuary, when the focus of the meditation at last came to bear on the Purple Ray, the riddle was solved. While contemplating, several of those present saw independently that the horizontal triangle had resolved itself into a three-sided pyramid with the figure of the Master Jesus at the apex in an ovoid of white light, from which the three Rays emanated, and that in the Third Ray was the Figure of the Virgin bearing the Cup.

This glyph balances perfectly. The Master Jesus is seen correctly placed on a higher plane, being at the apex of the pyramid and also at the centre of the Triangle in the Tiphareth position, and this is true symbolism. The placing of the Virgin Mary in Yesod is also correct symbolism, and yields most interesting results to meditation when the association chains begin to unfold.

The Figure of the Virgin has the indigo blue and purple colourings such as are seen in delphiniums, which are characteristic of Yesod. Her dark blue cloak was covered with silver stars and was the colour of the night sky; her under-dress was sky-blue and behind her head was the crescent moon, horns upward. At her left side grew a tall spray of Madonna lilies, with one unopened bud and two open flowers. This blue and silver Figure stood in the Ray of purple light holding the Cup.

The symbolism of all this becomes more interesting the more we contemplate it. Mary, Queen of Heaven, Star of the Sea, is the Eternal Mother, Ever Virgin. She is the ever-virgin unmanifest feminine principle of Binah, the Heavenly Isis; she is also Our Lady of Nature, ever-fecund. The two shades of blue of her garments signify her dual aspect. The Madonna lily is the western analogue of the lotus. Those who are familiar with Yoga symbolism will remember that when the lotus bud hangs downwards, it indicates that a chakra is in repose; and when the flower opens and turns its face upwards, it indicates that the Kundalini force is passing through that chakra.

> *9 June 1940 – Last week over 300,000 Allied troops were evacuated from Dunkirk. Britain now faces the imminent threat of invasion. Churchill vows, "We shall fight on the beaches ..."*

In the thirtieth letter, in the period leading up to the Summer Solstice, a new phase of the work is inaugurated. This is formulated in the development of a complete symbolic complex based upon the Tor at Glastonbury, and detailed instructions on how best to work within it.

LETTER 30
for June 9th 1940

It will be remembered that it was during the last meditations before the Whitsuntide holidays that we got the full formula of the triune, thus completing the first phase of our work. With the re-starting of our meditation circle, a new phase is opening, and we are now to build up the vision of the Mount of Illumination, beneath whose roots in earth the Cavern is set.

This is a traditional glyph of great importance. We saw it for the first time on the Sunday before Whitsuntide, but as no letter was sent out that week, no record of it was available for those who were not present.

As has been said before, the Cavern which is the starting point of all our meditations is conceived of as being situated beneath the Holy Mountain of the Illuminati. The Cavern is entered symbolically by a secret underground way through which alone can access be obtained to its higher aspects, symbolised by the Hall of Learning, conceived of as a great mediaeval library, and the Chapel of the Graal with its Watchtower. These are pictured as situated one above the other, a spiral stair set in the thickness of the rocky walls leading upwards. The Cavern is the meeting place in which the Brethren assemble. The Hall of Learning symbolises the acquirement of occult knowledge. The Chapel of the Graal is the place of spiritual power. Concerning the Watchtower which rises above it, not a great deal can be said at the moment, save that it is there that the silent Watcher, cowled and cloaked, keeps perpetual vigil.

In order to make use of this glyph, we commence the meditation as usual upon the Cross in the Cavern; then we imagine ourselves climbing the spiral staircase set in the thickness of the wall up to the Hall of Learning. A very interesting use can be made of this symbolic image. The student can imagine himself taking from the shelves with which he is surrounded a book bearing on some question in which he is specially interested, and turning its pages in imagination, try to read what is written therein. He will probably be able to see little more than symbols and a few short sentences; but he will find that in the immediate future, information on a desired subject, and understanding thereof, will come his way as if by chance. This method, of course, cannot be used for mundane matters.

Into the Chapel of the Graal we can go to kneel in devotion, to find peace, and to receive spiritual illumination. But if we join in the vigil on the Watchtower, we observe the workings of the invisible forces of both good and evil, and it is a position that exposes us to the risk of occult attack; therefore it is not for the inexperienced.

The Cavern is the secret place of meeting and of initiation. The concealed underground passage by which it is entered symbolises the cryptic, guarded, occult nature of the teaching. In the ordinary way only initiates of the Mysteries can gain access thereto, but in this time of national crisis and spiritual rebirth we have been able to be frank through those who are working with us, relying upon the nature of the forces that operate through these symbols to reject the unworthy. So far our confidence has been amply justified.

The work for the next week will be to build up the glyph of the three chambered Mount of Illumination and to become familiar with the practice of going from storey to storey by way of the winding stair. Those who care to do so can essay the Watchtower, but they may find that the winds of astral force are blowing full gale, and the silent Watcher is a formidable figure.

16 June 1940 – German forces pour through the Maginot Line. Allied forces evacuate from Brest and St Malo.

The thirty-first letter gives a résumé of the development of the work so far, together with a little more detail on the practicalities of working with symbolism. And lest any should have any doubts upon the matter, Dion Fortune sets out in clear terms that the performance of esoteric work is no excuse for lack of commitment to outer work in the world. In fact that to neglect the call of physical plane demands is likely to break the circuit, thus rendering any intended Inner Plane work ineffective.

LETTER 31
for June 16th 1940

Those who have followed the course of our work from its beginning and seen its growth, know that it was not a thing which had been thought out and planned by human intelligence, but that it was gradually unfolded in a series of visions or revelations, each leading on to the next.

The starting point was the simple Cross with Circle, which symbolises salvation through knowledge. From it quickly developed the Rose Cross, famous in tradition, of which so little is known historically. Then came the formulation of the Cavern beneath the Mount of Illumination where certain of the Elder Brethren came to meet us in the Light.

Thus was established the astral meeting place for our work. Those who have built up the vision in their imagination till it has become a reality for them, can use it as a taking-off place for all manner of work on the Inner Planes, for thus, by means of the establishment of a thought-out form on the astral plane and a chain of associated ideas leading thereto, are gates of ingress to the Unseen established.

Once this gateway and meeting place has been formulated, it can be used for all manner of purposes. During the long pause before the battle was joined, we made use of it to build up a glyph which revealed to us the whole scope and scheme of the plan to which we were working, and of which our war effort constitutes the opening phase. It will be found very useful to have recourse to this glyph in meditation whenever the way seems dark or doubtful, or the burden of war weighs heavy upon us. It is as if a traveller toiling through a dense forest climbed to the topmost branches of a high tree and saw the whole landscape through which he must make his way spread out before him.

With the sudden intensification of the war, this glyph was put aside and our efforts concentrated on the bringing through of power and the war effort. Then came a curious development, and we found ourselves being led from level to level of the Mount of Illumination, and passing through the Hall of Learning and the Chapel of the Graal.

Both these mystical representations have their special uses. If we imagine ourselves to be in the Hall of Learning, we can use the contacts thus made to acquire technical occult knowledge in the manner described in a previous letter. If we picture ourselves in the Chapel of the Graal, we find that we are immediately in touch with the most potent spiritual forces. If we mount yet higher, and come out on the Watchtower, we shall discover powers of vision are available to us, but that strong and contending forces will beat upon us.

On Sunday, in the sanctuary, we found that the strongest contacts were those of the Chapel of the Graal, and that from the vision there received, there came a very brilliant and very pure spiritual illumination. In the time of effort and testing that we are passing through, spiritual strength is needed, both by us as individuals and by the nation as a whole. It is through spiritual strength that we shall triumph over the brute force that opposes us. Nazism has physical and astral and mental powers, but it has no spiritual contacts, hence its lack of all ethical standards and its complete irresponsibility.

We, on our part, have the spiritual forces of the cosmos behind us. For these we have to make channels through our own natures; we are, in fact, the channels of their manifestation in exact proportion to our realisation of them. As soon as these channels are opened into any plane or sphere, the forces will build forms there for themselves. We do not have to toil at the form-building; we simply have to win the realisations and hold them steadily; then the forces do their own work.

We shall see, in the most amazing way, results follow realisation. This does not mean that, if we do Inner Plane work we have no need to bear our share in the national effort. There will always be those whose Inner Plane work occupies their whole time, but they are few. Having done our meditations, we should return refreshed and inspired to do with all our might whatever tasks lie to hand. From our Inner Plane contacts we draw strength and inspiration; in our work on the physical plane we give expression to what we have received. It is not enough to make contact and receive inspiration. The inspiration will soon dry up unless it flows through us, ever renewing itself in flowing. For those who have the deeper knowledge, participation in the national war effort is a sacramental act whereby the power that has been drawn down is put in circuit. Break the circuit, and the power ceases to flow.

> *23 June 1940 – Accompanied by his architect, Albert Speer, Adolf Hitler today toured the great monuments of German-held Paris.*

There are certain prophetic elements to be found in some of the symbolic meditations, as is apparent in the next two letters.

LETTER 32
for June 23rd 1940

Last Sunday the meditation in the Sanctuary was very powerful – one of the most powerful I have ever known. A beam of diamond light came down spontaneously as soon as the Elder Brethren had come to meet us, and this beam was then directed towards France, so that it lay like a barrier right across that country into Africa, and seemed to be supporting the allied armies. Not until the meditation was over did I realise that Sunday was the day set aside as a day of prayer for France. In all my experience of occult work I have never seen anything more tangible than that beam of force.

In connection with the marked change of feeling in America, I would like to remind my readers that three weeks ago we saw in our meditation a beam of force go out and touch the United States. It will also be recalled that the entry of Italy into the war was announced a fortnight before it occurred. We do not point to these things in a spirit of boasting, but because they give us confidence in the reality and power of what we are doing.

LETTER 33
for June 30th 1940

In our last letter an account was given of the beam of power that was seen going from England across France to rest on North Africa. Since then, France as an independent nation has ceased to exist, but the African colonies of France have announced their determination not to yield. I take little stock in prophecy, but I was puzzled at the time that the ray of power that was being sent out to France did not appear to rest on France, but passed on to Africa. Now we know the unhappy significance of that vision.

7 July 1940 – In the Mediterranean and Africa, British forces destroy the French fleet to stop them falling into German hands.

Another dimension to the work is discussed in the thirty-fourth letter, the direct use of occult methods to sap morale and influence the group souls of the nations.

LETTER 34
for July 7th 1940

If we as a nation make ourselves a channel of cosmic law through realisation of the spiritual nature of the struggle we are waging, we become the channel for the manifestation of the power of God, and the stars in their courses will literally fight for us, as they did in the weather conditions attending the evacuation of the B.E.F. from Dunkirk, when the storm and the calm fell exactly as needed and even the military authorities talked of a miracle.

But the weapons of our adversary's warfare are not wholly carnal, either. We have seen the peculiar way in which the morale of nation after nation falls suddenly to pieces when courage and loyalty could have saved the day. This is due to a form of Fifth Column activity which has not received the recognition which is its due. In fact, so specialised and unrecognised is it that we might justly talk of Sixth Column activities. These activities are purely mental; Hitler's well known psychological methods form part of them, but there is more to it than that.

We are, in my opinion, dealing with definite occult forces being used telepathically on the group souls of nations, and finding channels of expression through the subconsciousness of susceptible people who lack spiritual principles. I am satisfied that we are not the only group that is broadcasting to the subconscious mind of the race; and that just as we have found ourselves able to pour in spiritual power, others, using similar methods, are trying to undermine our morale.

This is a serious matter, and we must not shrink from facing it. But, on the other hand, nine months' steady work lies behind us. We have built up something very strong and definite. Those who come to meet us in the Light have established their contacts with the group mind of the race, and I believe the situation to be well in hand provided we do not allow our selves to relax our vigilance or let ourselves be deceived by specious pseudo-idealism. There is not room for Nazism and democratic civilisation on the same globe, and one or the other will have to get off it – let us bear this constantly in mind when subtle attacks come to be made on our morale, as they certainly will be when force proves expensive.

There is one sure protection against this subversive telepathy – spiritual principles, clearly realised ideals, and dedication to them, even unto death. In order to counteract this telepathic undermining of the group mind, which showed itself first in complacency and unsuspiciousness of the obvious, and from which we have only recently awakened, we must have not merely physical courage, but a spiritual basis to our morale that shall lift us right above the level on which subversive telepathy works. We must take our stand on spiritual values in national life, and then no fear of destruction of property or the sufferings of individuals will cause us to sell our birthright for a scrap of paper.

4 August 1940 – The German air offensive against Britain is postponed because of bad weather conditions.

Deeper implications of the unseen warfare are developed in the thirty-sixth letter. There is a deeply positive optimism in Dion Fortune's remarks this time, and it may be recalled that these were written in the August of 1940, the time of the Battle of Britain, the country's finest and darkest hour, when, in Churchill's later words, so many owed so much to so few.

LETTER 36
for August 4th 1940

There is something very strange about this war. The nations that have been subjugated were not beaten in the field, they fell to treachery and internal corruption; to lack of morale and lack of the will to victory. The key to their fall may be found in the words: "he who would save his life shall lose it, and he who will lose his life for My sake shall find it." Those who prefer security to freedom have lost both.

England stands alone and happy. All war gloom has gone. There is confidence in the future and pride in the present. Power is rising within us like a tide. The inflowing of a new life impulse is making itself felt.

8 September 1940 – In London, 412 people die and 747 are injured in bombing attacks. Hitler delays his invasion plans.

As the aerial warfare over London was hotting up, in the forty-first letter we find Dion Fortune giving advice on how to meditate and maintain a serene mind in the midst of distractions and dangers. Although few students may have to put up with the conditions of war she describes, nonetheless the advice remains sound for coping with the lesser trials of life that seem to conspire against esoteric work.

LETTER 41
for September 8th 1940

There is only one way to keep quiet and serene under bombardment – to be prepared to lay down your life for your country if necessary. Once that eventuality is accepted, one abrogates one's civilian mentality, and the passivity and helplessness that go with it. Regard the warning wail of the siren as an 'alert' not as a 'retreat', unless specifically ordered to get out of the way. Carry on as near normal as you can without running undue risks.

So much for the end to be aimed at. Let us now consider how, from the esoteric point of view, it can best be achieved. People should, by now, have got used to being wailed at, and have learnt to judge by the familiar sounds how far the threatened danger is immediate. Then, having taken what precautions you can, accept the residue of the risk with fortitude. When the actual bombing starts, or the sound of gunfire is alarmingly near, go into meditation, if possible assuming the meditation posture. Now, this may seem impossible of achievement during the din of a raid, and so it would be for the untrained mind; but if preparations have been made in advance, it will prove unexpectedly easy, for the stress of an air raid heightens psychic perception, and many a person will witness the parting of the Veil and see into the Unseen who, under normal conditions, might have to work long before they achieved such an experience.

Each person should compose for themselves a short mantram, or rhythmical sentence of invocation of the Masters to be present and protect, and should repeat it silently like a litany until the mental turmoil ceases and it is possible to perform meditation proper. If the turmoil can be stilled even for a few seconds, it will be possible to pick up the inner contacts with every probability of vision opening and enabling us to see the work going on the Inner Planes, for the Invisible Helpers come very close to earth at these times.

Try and make contact with these, not in order that they may protect you, but that you may co-operate with them in helping those around you. You will find them very ready to avail themselves of your co-operation, for their problem is to establish contact with the people they are trying to help, who, not being psychic, are very difficult for them to influence. It is in such circumstances as these that the value of steady, regular meditation shows itself, and if you have learnt to discipline the mind and enter into the quiet amid the distractions of everyday life, which so many people allege prevent them from meditation, then you may have the great experience of seeing the heavens open when the stress of the moment has given just that extra turn of the screw that makes consciousness change gear.

During our meditation on Sunday, we were conscious of the coming of a Messenger, and it is probable that steps are being taken to establish contact and co-operation with those who work as Invisible Helpers in close touch with the earth-sphere. It would therefore be well, when danger threatens, to formulate the Rose Cross in the same way that you would put up a notice indicating that there is a stirrup pump in your house, so that any Invisible Helper who is working in your environment may know where to look for co-operation, but to remember that to do this involves willingness to sacrifice yourself if necessary.

15 September 1940 – Following extensive losses of aircraft in the "Battle of Britain", Hitler delays his invasion plans indefinitely. However, the Blitz continues.

The theme of Inner Plane cooperation and protection is developed in the next letter also.

LETTER 42
for September 15th 1940

Under stress, the directing intelligence is apt to be abrogated, and the subconsciousness to come up and take charge. Then it is that the regular practice of meditation shows its value, for we find that what comes up is a disciplined subconsciousness, filled with the meditation images that we have so laboriously impressed upon it during the long months of systematic work that lie behind us. Automatically the images appear and do their work, holding us steady and on our contact, even as we, in the patient routine of daily meditation, have practised holding them steady.

But in addition to our physical plane precautions, let us have our meditation scheme planned and ready, and set it going with invocation and visualisation as soon as danger threatens. We can plan to meet the Masters in the Cavern, or retire into the Chapel of the Graal, and a power will come down upon us that will radiate to all around us, steadying the atmosphere and bringing calm and relaxation of tension, as some of our members have already proved. Until we begin to use these methods under conditions of stress, we have no idea what can be done with them. We fear to be credulous, or to be deceiving our selves, but faith is necessary for any form of work that depends on mind power. Let us act 'as if' what we want to believe is true, and we shall find that we have very likely brought it into manifestation. The results that can be achieved in this way have to be seen to be believed.

Advice on meditation under difficulties was soon put to the test as can be seen in the opening paragraph of the forty-third letter.

LETTER 43
for September 22nd 1940

Our meditation this week was conducted to the accompaniment of a dogfight at a low altitude immediately overhead and an incendiary bomb next door but one, and we have never had a more absolute sense of peace and power.

And by the end of the following month the outer and inner conflict had become very closely interconnected, as letter forty-seven reveals.

LETTER 47
for October 20th 1940

At 3 Queensborough Terrace we had on Saturday night the experience of being straddled by a stick of four bombs, our head-quarters just fitting neatly into the middle of them, and, though well shaken, escaping all damage. As the crashes drew nearer and nearer amid a concentration of A.A. [anti-aircraft] fire, the conditions were such that the inner and outer planes seemed to merge, and it was possible to see the Invisible Helpers at work as innumerable shadowy presences. There were also presences of a much higher and more intellectual grade who seemed to be holding lines of power taut under great tension. Over all was the iridescent dome of protection guarded by great angelic presences. These are among the things we have been visualising and building on the astral, and at the moment of testing it was a wonderful experience to see how potent and tangible they were. The stick of bombs fell one after the other in roads and gardens and there were no casualties. This is the second time that this has happened in our immediate vicinity. That there are powerful forces at work can hardly be denied.

Our friends can help with the work of protection by frequent and regular invocation. Knowing that many must give their lives and sacrifice their property before the war is won, we have no right to ask that we should be spared and others taken; and indeed if we do ask it there appears to be no particular reason why the prayer should be granted. But if we have dedicated our lives to the service of the Masters then we are entitled to call down the power that shall protect us while we do the work we have undertaken, just as military headquarters are protected by defences. We have offered our lives, and may be taken at our word in the course of our work; but until that time comes, we need conditions under which we can work efficiently, and it is a part of that work that we should build ourselves defences.

Therefore let our friends, and their friends, invoke for the protection of the dedicated priesthood and the dedicated places in the name of the Holy Rosicrucian Order, for calling upon the Great Ones of that Order we make contact with them and open channels for their power to manifest on the physical plane.

Indeed, at the moment of clear vision during the bombing, it was conveyed to us that the great and urgent need at the moment was for such channels to be opened freely and that we should be bold in making and invoking these contacts, not diffident and circumspect. It is with this great Symbol that we have worked all these months, and we must make increasing use of it.

During the past year it will be recalled that we worked for two things; the morale of the nation and a new world order when peace shall be declared. Now that the testing has come, the morale of the nation has proved itself to be beyond praise and the idea of regeneration and reconstruction is discussed on all hands. A new phase of our work is opening up and will be made clear in the course of the next weeks.

27 October 1940 – During October, 6350 civilians die, and 8700 are injured in bombing raids.

And despite the heroic and dedicated building of protective images the roof fell in, literally, in the following week, as Dion Fortune wryly explains.

LETTER 48
for October 27th 1940

In our last letter we asked our members and friends to invoke for the protection of 3 Queensborough Terrace, and in this letter we have the ironical task of informing them that we have been bombed out of it, though without casualties; so it may be maintained that the invocation was at least a partial success, though your Leader and her Librarian look like a couple of sweeps owing to a difference of opinion with the roof, which fell in on them, but tactfully refrained from hitting them.

It has often been alleged that Dion Fortune is a Black Occultist, and we regretfully admit that the allegation can no longer be denied; however it is hoped that soap and water will restore her to the Right Hand Path and her students will once more be able to hold up their heads before a world always too ready to think the worst.

The meditation meeting was held as usual despite the "incident", and there was a wonderful sense of serene peace. "Shocked" people from next door were resting in the office, and they remarked on the peacefulness of the atmosphere.

Later in the day the house was pronounced unsafe, and we had to evacuate; this is thought to be a precautionary measure, however, as there are no cracks in the walls. All the resident members are safely installed in our annexe in the lower maisonette at No. 21a Queensborough Terrace; phone: BAY 6853. Everyone is serene and cheerful and quite unaffected by their experience, and we feel it may be fairly said that the method of mind training and thought control taught in the Fraternity has proved its value.

Our friends may like to know that although everything was thrown off the altar in the sanctuary, the statue of the Risen Christ remained standing on its pedestal, though shifted to the very edge.

The worst had passed within a couple of weeks however, and things were getting back to normal.

LETTER 50
for November 19th 1940

We have no further adventures to recount, we are grateful to say, save that by the time this letter is received 3 Queensborough Terrace will have been made weatherproof and we shall be contemplating the problem of getting it clean – unless, of course, we are re-bombed in the meantime.

> *24 November 1940 – In Berlin this week, the German High Command finishes its plans for the invasion of Russia – Operation Barbarossa.*

The letters that follow, just over a year after the outbreak of war, take on a subtle change of function. They start to lay down general principles for the reconstruction of the country and the Mysteries when hostilities are over. In letter fifty-one, for example, there is a description of the initiate.

LETTER 51
for November 24th 1940

The initiate works by what he is rather than by what he does, and the higher his grade, the more passive he appears to be on the physical plane. Should he take action thereon, he abrogates his power to operate on the Inner Planes, for one cannot be positive on both planes simultaneously.

The initiate is what he is by virtue of the possession of certain basic qualities which are perfected by training. Firstly, he must not be self-centred, but in sympathetic relationship with all manifested life. Those who seek occult knowledge in order that it may help them in their troubles are a step nearer the Path than those who seek it to satisfy a desire for knowledge, and these are in their turn a step further than those who seek it as a means to power, but they are not yet on the Path. They may, it is true, receive help if there is a prospect that, being helped, they will make spiritual growth, but the work of those who train for initiation is not to help people, but to equip them to be helpers. Who would enrol as air raid wardens casualties lying on stretchers? So those who seek occult knowledge in order to find help in their troubles are apt to find the dose too strong. Just as the ancient Hebrew law required the priests of the Temple to be without maim or defect, so those who present themselves for the higher initiations must have worked out their personal troubles and find equilibrium and freedom before they dare to come to the altar. They are helped to do this work in the Outer Court and the Lesser Mysteries, but they may not enter upon the Greater Mysteries until it is done.

The initiate of the Greater Mysteries is known by his serenity and impersonal attitude in all the relations of life. He knows how to be still and let the powers he has set in motion carry out the work. He knows how to await the ripening of souls and not force a premature development by personal pressure. The initiate never goes about doing good; he never trespasses uninvited upon spiritual privacy of another. He acts by what he is, not by what he does. He works on himself, makes something of himself, and then the forces that radiate from him without effort on his part bless and illuminate. If he is calm, he calms his environment. If he has wisdom, those who are in his company unconsciously take on his attitude and he has no need to proffer unsolicited advice. Because he knows the reality of eternity, he is content to let time do its work. He is characterised by two things: the power to be still and wait, and the power to stand absolutely alone. Until we know how to be still, mentally as well as physically, we cannot handle power; and until we know how to stand absolutely alone in perfect equilibrium and contentment, we cannot accomplish the works that are done in polarity. Finally, the initiate is prepared to work without seeing results, playing his part on the Great Plan that unfolds through the ages of planetary time.

12 January 1941 – The US Congress finally passes the "Lease and Lend" Bill which allows President Roosevelt to supply Britain with massive amounts of military aid.

The task of the initiate is further developed in the fifty-sixth letter.

LETTER 56
for January 12th 1941

It is our task, as esotericists, recognising causation in the Unseen and end results only on the plane of matter, to formulate in our minds the plan and concept of the new order of things that is being brought to birth on the circuit of cosmic time. The process goes through three phases. First, as Leader, I have to obtain the realisations and teachings; then as a group we have to formulate them in meditation; finally, the individual members of the group have got to work them out in their own lives. Thus is the group mind of the race "inoculated" with the new concepts. Inoculation of the group mind can only take place when members of that group mind receive and act upon the ideas; aliens cannot inoculate it. It will be noted that Hitler has always undermined a country through its own citizens, not through German-born agents...

In order to alter environment by mind power we commence by realising the infinite and eternal energy of the Great Unmanifest. Each of us has as our nucleus of organisation a spark of Unmanifest Life, and this Divine Spark is as inexhaustible in its energy as a grain of radium. By means of realisation and formulation we build the machinery of its manifestation in our being provided formulation is according to practicable cosmic law, and not wild fantasy. But just as an inventor may conceive a wonderful scheme which may not be mechanically practicable, so we may conceive some life ideal which is not according to cosmic law and consequently is unworkable. But if our scheme is feasible, life will flow into it and realise it.

Circumstances are formed by personality to a far greater degree than we realise. According to our natures we contact or avoid the influences of our environment. Change the personality, and it will 'tune in' to a different set of environmental influences. We see this in the case of a man who takes to drink; we see it in the case of a man who "gets religion"; we could see it in our own case if we set to work systematically to use mind power. The initiate builds himself a "mask" or "persona", to use the technical term of the Mysteries. He does this by imagining himself in an imaginary mirror in that likeness. His mental image will affect not only his own consciousness, but the attitude of others towards him, and their attitude towards him will reinforce the effect on himself of his own mental work. Let us practise and experiment along those lines in order that we may shadow forth the shape of things to come.

26 January 1941 – In the desert war in Africa, British and Australian troops take Tobruk and continue to push back the Italian fascists on all fronts.

There are nuggets of information on other practicalities of occultism, in letter fifty-eight, on the method of using symbols.

LETTER 58
for January 26th 1941

As all who have worked with us know we work with a Pictorial system of group meditation, visualising images – scenes instead of the more usual metaphysical contemplation. Our method is not without precedent, however, for it is that of the Egyptian and Tibetan initiates and is known in the Western world as the Composition of Place, taught by Ignatius Loyola in his Exercises. It is, in fact, both of these things, and they are mutually re-enforcing, not mutually exclusive.

The use of symbols, and especially the combination of the symbols into a glyph, needs to be thoroughly understood if it is to be applied intelligently and its full scope rendered available. In order to obtain real insight into its nature we must go back to the beginning of things and see upon what it is based and how it came into being. Those who have studied *The Cosmic Doctrine* will recognise the principles to which it relates.

The beginning of manifestation may best be represented under the concept of currents of force moving through space. These by their inherent nature are organised in course of cosmic time into the Rings and the Rays. Those again became co-ordinated into vortices of force that possessed stability. The vortices in their turn became organised into constellations of units of stability. The details of the process of the evolution of form-substance cannot be entered upon here, and this brief outline must suffice.

Each phase of evolution produced a particular type of organisation of the units of pre-matter; a phase built up its basic units by co-ordinating the units of its predecessor, which in their turn had been built up out of the units of the earlier phases. Only a modicum of each form of basic substance was utilised, so that the greater part remained, co-existing with both earlier and later forms of development, just as in a lake may be found all forms of life, from unicellular protozoa through the worm, insect, fish and frog types, up to the waterbirds and others; thus every phase of the evolution of animal life is represented. We must never think of the planes as lying in layers, one above the other, but as interpenetrating and built up into each other's substance, so that if one breaks up the substance of a plane, it disintegrates into its component parts as the substance developed during an earlier phase of evolution.

All manifestation on all planes is thus built up, and so is our own fourfold being. Our vehicles of consciousness are formed of the substance of the corresponding plane, just as our physical bodies are formed of calcium, iron, phosphorus and other elements of the physical plane; and just as there is a constant circulation of substance between our bodies and the world of matter through the intake of food and the output of energy, so is there a similar circulation between our subtle vehicles, and their conditions influence us.

Civilised man, however, has concentrated on the focus of consciousness to the exclusion of all else, and his subtler powers of perception have, in consequence, been overlaid by superficial accretions and atrophied for lack of use. Primitive man, however, was aware of the subtle sensations arising from the influence of the Inner Planes impinging on the substance drawn therefrom that was incorporated in his being. Seeking to understand the nature of that of which he was thus made aware, he projected his own nature upon it, attributing by analogy his own methods and motives to the intangible life he felt around him. In this he was probably approximately correct, for it may be presumed that the same principles of organisation prevail throughout the long history of evolution. Primitive man represented his concepts of the world order in pictorial form and dramatised them into myths. Such pictures and myths consequently correspond to conditions of pre-matter with which he was much better acquainted than we are; and when we want to contact these levels of existence, we shall avail ourselves of his methods, employing the subconscious mechanisms which correspond to the primitive phase of mental development. Thus we set flowing currents of force between the subtler aspects of our own four-fold being and the corresponding levels of the Inner Planes.

In order to achieve this, we connect up the conscious mind with the subconscious by filling the conscious mind with the kind of contents that occupy subconsciousness and imitating its methods. Thus we take one or another of the racial myths that have come down to us traditionally from pre-history, and we dramatise it either in meditation as Composition of Place and Colloquy, to borrow the terminology of St Ignatius, or as a dramatic ritual or Mystery play; when we do this, consciousness, subconsciousness and superconsciousness are brought into alignment, and there is a straight run through of cosmic force.

Shortly afterwards, in her sixty-fifth letter, Dion Fortune gives quite specific instructions on the working of astral magic as a force in the general war effort. This is sparked by various publications of the time that sought to foster an attitude of hatred toward the German people. While she considers such an attitude unregenerate and unwise, she concedes that there might be a special problem with the racial soul of Germany.

Of two authorities she cites, Sir Robert Vansittart stressed what he saw as an undying hatred of the average German for England, despite other English visitors to pre-war Germany having reported the kindliness and friendliness of individual Germans. While Lewis Spence, in his book *The Occult Causes of the War* expressed a belief in an organised force of intelligent occult evil active in Germany that was definitely anti-Christian.

Dion Fortune draws her own conclusions, which she here expresses, together with an invitation to her group to do something about it.

LETTER 65
for March 16th 1941

Personally, I think it is a blind force, not an intelligent one, and that it finds a channel through the personalities of unregenerate human beings who provide the intelligence it does not possess. I conceive of this dark influence as the accumulation of evil thought-forms in the group mind of the race and place; an evil heritage that has come down undispersed from the dawn of German history and even earlier, and that overshadows the crowd psychology of the German people to this day. There can be no reform of Germany as a political factor in Europe until this dark psychic heritage that contaminates her is dispersed and neutralised. Propaganda that appeals to the conscious minds of Germans is as futile as argument with a lunatic, for it is not in their power to respond. There is one thing, and one thing only that can disperse this dark cloud of ancestral evil and set the souls of Germans free, and that is the Power of the Christ, and we must bring this power to bear.

Let us visualise Germany as a vast marsh of human helplessness and ignorance covered by the thick black cloud of ancient evil; the sunlight of the Christ cannot reach it to dry up the stagnant waters and give it health and fertility until this cloud has been dispersed. Then let us see the Angels of the Lord hovering over it and directing lightning flashes at it from the points of their swords. These flashes cause thunder-storms to break out in the cloud; rifts appear, the cloud begins to break up and the Sunshine of Christ shines throughout the land beneath. This method, if persisted with, will soon disperse the cloud, and remember we are striking at the cloud, and not the land beneath it. Once this is dispersed, the healing sunshine will do the rest.

Seventy years on, we might pause to reflect whether these remarks about Germany could equally be said about most nations of the world, including our own. And whether a similar remedy might not be appropriate.

Two weeks later Dion Fortune analysed the esoteric forces set in motion by the recent National Day of Prayer. These public events were observed throughout the war, and like all movements involving mass psychology, of whatever kind, had their esoteric implications.

LETTER 67
for March 30th 1941

The national day of prayer which has just passed will undoubtedly have let loose powerful forces in the atmosphere of the race. We must not be surprised if these forces prove destructive as well as constructive, for greater potencies are wielded in this manner than is realised by those setting them in motion. The destruction thus caused, though disruptive at the time, is by no means evil unless it is excessive; for although changes must come, they should not be introduced so drastically as to disrupt organic national life and cause the spiritual equivalent of surgical shock. This is a thing which is apt to happen when spiritual force is set in motion by the uninitiated, who do not realise that it is a two-edged weapon and to be used with discrimination, for it is possible to bring more redemptive power to bear on the soul than the mind can stand; hence the wisdom of the custom that sets aside Lent as the period of repentance and closes the door of the subjective purgatory on Easter Eve.

We who have knowledge of the laws and nature of the Inner Planes and the forces that operate thereon should use our knowledge of these powers to assist in directing and controlling what might otherwise be a blind ebullition of energy, well intentioned but undirected. Let us seek the cooperation of Those who come to us in the Light in order that these blind spiritual forces may be intelligently directed.

6 April 1941 – Erwin Rommel's Afrika Korps rapidly advances across North Africa re-taking ground recently won by British troops.

In the letter that follows Dion Fortune describes in some detail the symbolism that the group continues to build. In this spontaneous description of images we see a particular application of the technique that has come to be called "path working".

LETTER 68
for April 6th 1941

The work of our meditation group which meets on Sundays at No. 3 Queensborough Terrace falls into two divisions. Firstly the teaching and instruction that is given in the lecture, which forms the basis of the subsequent letters; secondly, the group meditation which uses the symbol of the Many-coloured Rose upon the Cross of Gold as a key-call and the Cavern under the Hill of Vision as a meeting place.

The meditation follows no fixed plan once contact has been established as described above, but what is seen is reported in exactly the same manner as a BBC running commentary on some event. This enables all present to share in the vision and trains them in the technique of seership.

Those who have been with us from the commencement of this work know how gradually the Vision has built up through all its phases, from the Cavern to the Watchtower and the Vision within the Vision of the Three-fold Glyph. They will also recall that it never varies; that whatever has once been formulated always re-formulates in precisely the same way. When, therefore, we have to report a change in the vision, it will be realised that this is a event of great significance.

Last Sunday marked the commencement of the new tide which begins to flow with the new moon of the Vernal Equinox. The meditation began as usual, with the formulation of the Rose Cross and Cave, and then, with the appearance of Those who come to meet us in the Light, the change occurred. As usual, They took charge of vision, and, as They have so often done before, led us by the winding stair in the thickness of rock up into the Hall of Learning. Arrived there, They reformulated once more the Rose Cross and made with us a circle about it. Then the light began to brighten, and the books lining the walls, which had hitherto always been dimly seen amid the shadows, appeared for a few moments in bright golden light so that the details of their bindings could be seen whichever way one looked.

Then the light faded that had shone on the books, and the Masters led us once more down to the winding stair into the Cavern; but when we arrived, the Cross was no longer there, for it had been transferred to the Hall of Learning.

We re-formed our circle as usual, however, and then Those who come to us in the Light, the Regents of the Rays, moved backwards as if in a Ritual, and through their ranks came seven others, Their subordinates, each wearing the robes of his Ray. These we were given to understand were the Teaching Masters.

What the significance of this vision may be remains to be seen. Certain tentative interpretations may be formulated, however. The Many-coloured Rose upon the Cross of Gold is the key to all Mysteries because each Petal has a significance which is interpreted by means of the Tree of Life. The Tree of Life is fully explained in *The Mystical Qabalah*, and whoso has a correctly coloured Rose can see at once how to place the symbols on it and interpret their meaning.

The colouring of the Paths and the colouring of the Petals, however, is only known to initiates. Nor is it enough to know the colourings; the Paths have to be trodden in mystical experience before the Petals become coloured. Some who have shared in the Vision may have seen the Rose distinctly, and some may not, but every one of its Petals has a precise significance in the Mysteries.

The Hall of Learning lined with volumes containing the secrets of the Ancient Wisdom symbolises the interpretation to the conscious mind of the higher knowledge. This interpretation is accomplished by means of analogy and the clearest clues are found in physics taken in conjunction with psychology. The fact that we were shown the Rose Cross transferred to the Hall of Learning may perhaps be taken to mean that definite teaching will be vouchsafed to those who have worked so faithfully.

The subsequent scene on the return to the Cavern bears out this view. The Regents of the Rays do not teach; They simply transmit power and direct its working. The Teaching Masters are of a much lower grade in the Hierarchy. The fact that the Regents stepped back and let the Teaching Masters come through to us may perhaps mean that whereas the group have had hitherto to make use of symbols without knowing their meaning, the meaning will now be communicated to them.

> *27 April 1941 – As German troops move steadily into Greece, the Greek government escapes to Crete.*

A couple of weeks later Dion Fortune shows the way dedicated group meditation links in to the national consciousness and thence leads to action in the outer world.

LETTER 70
for April 27th 1941

Inner Plane work always moves a tide ahead of physical plane activities; consequently we in our group work do not concern ourselves with the critical phases of the war that are being passed through in Libya and the Balkans, on the Atlantic and in the blitzed towns. Our work on national morale is done, and our work on the spiritual significance of the war has concluded its first phase and enters upon its second.

Let us remind ourselves once more of the way in which our work is done. The innumerable individuals who make up a nation share a common subconsciousness below the personal subconsciousness of each one; this is called the racial or collective subconsciousness, and it plays a very important part in both individual and national life. Here abide the archetypal ideas that are common to each one of us and that we never have to learn. These give rise to myth and symbol, dream, poetry and art.

It is this level of the subconsciousness that is appealed to by national heroes; it is this level that is manipulated by spellbinding demagogues. It is here that the trend and limitations of the national character are determined, and from here that its inspiration is drawn.

We work by inoculating the collective subconsciousness of the race with certain archetypal ideas which have been communicated to us psychically in the course of our group meditation. Those who have been with us since the formation of our meditation group will recall how these have been gradually built up.

It may pertinently be asked in this connection whether others as well as ourselves cannot also work along these lines, both for good and evil. The answer is that they can. There may be other groups as well as ourselves co-operating with Those who come to see us in the Light. Equally, the same methods could be used to infiltrate the group mind for Fifth Column purposes, and there is more than a possibility that this is being done. How, then, amid this war of ideas, can we be sure that right will prevail?

The collective subconsciousness of the race has its own well-defined characterisations and temperament which resist the introduction of anything alien thereto. There is, moreover, intelligent guidance on the part of those we call Masters, and behind them, the Racial Archangels, who take an active part in protecting the soul of the race against trespassing. It is from this source that we receive the archetypal ideas with which we work, and our task is to introduce these into the collective consciousness of our race by formulating them in our own individual consciousnesses, in such a manner that they reach the racial subconsciousness via the corresponding level in our own minds.

This we achieve by coming together in a group and forming a miniature collective subconsciousness and meditating with the imagination. Now, the imagination is the myth-making faculty, and when we use it, we are using our minds in the subconscious manner, and thus obtain access to the subconscious levels. We have been engaged in creating a myth which by its nature is in harmony with our national tradition. This is readily accepted by the group mind of the race and spreads and multiplies in it like yeast as mind after mind that has the capacity for such ideas picks them up subconsciously and brings them through into consciousness and begins to ponder them.

After the pondering will come the planned action, but that does not concern us. It is a work for experts, each in his own sphere. These experts will be men who combine action and idealism, and such are becoming increasingly common in this new epoch that is the work of the mystics and psychics. These messages are transmitted through the beings of the Racial Archangels, formulated in the consciousness of the Masters of our Ray and race, and given concrete expression in the lives of those who, like ourselves, undertake to work with the Masters.

The link between the mystic and the man of action is the philosophic intellect, and part of our work is to reduce these ideas to terms that the intellect can apprehend. This is my personal task, and for its execution I need the support of a group of workers, not large in numbers, but highly trained, closely knit by mutual sympathy, and dedicated lives.

> *25 May 1941 – This week, after heavy fighting, Crete falls to the Germans.*

At the end of the above letter we find an announcement that the Fraternity is resuming its "Outer Court" teaching activities, and that particulars of the study courses may once more be obtained from the Secretary. And at the end of May we find a detailed résumé of the work of the meditation group together with a forecast of the importance of the Mysteries in the years to come.

LETTER 74
for May 25th 1941

In order to avoid falling into superstition in occult work, it is necessary to have a clear understanding of the technique that is being employed, which rests upon a psychological basis.

We hold our group meditation at a fixed time – 12:15 on Sunday mornings, the hour being chosen for its general convenience and for no other reason. At the appointed time the people present assume the position seen in Egyptian statues, feet and knees parallel but not in contact, and hands laid flat along thighs. This is the best position for group working because it leaves the terminals of the human magnetic circuit open for the pooling of force, whereas an attitude with feet crossed and hands folded is best for private meditation because it conserves magnetic force. They then tranquillise the breathing to a fourfold rhythm in which the pauses between the breaths are the same as the lengths of the breaths. This is done by counting the same number of heart-beats on the inbreathing, the pause with full lungs, and the outbreathing, and the pause with empty lungs, all of which is done without effort, the aim being to promote rhythm, not lung expansion.

The leader of the group then seals the place of meeting with the Ritual of the Lesser Pentagram, which invokes the Four Holy Names of God and the four Archangels at the four points of the compass.

Meditation commences with the visualisation of the Many-petalled Rose upon a Cross of Gold. This form of Rose-cross is chosen in preference to the simpler form, which consists of a five-petalled red rose on a black Calvary cross standing on a base of three steps. This latter form is the Mystical Rose-cross. The three steps represent the grades of initiation through life experience; the black Calvary cross represents initiation through sacrifice, and the five-petalled red Tudor rose with a golden centre, re-birth through illumination. This form of the cross is used by those who tread the Devotional Path, which in the East is known as Bhakti Yoga, or illumination through love and devotion. In our work, however, we use the more complex form of the Rose-cross, which represents initiation through knowledge. In this form the cross is of gold; the limbs terminate in a trefoil, indicating the synthesis of the Pairs of Opposites in a Functional Third, which is the formula of the operation of cosmic force.

The Many-petalled Rose in the centre consists of three concentric circles of petals around a diamond heart. The first circle consists of three petals, representing the threefold nature of manifestation as previously described, and coloured in the three primary colours of red, yellow and blue; the next circle consists of seven petals coloured according to the seven rays of the spectrum, and representing the seven planets. The third ring consists of twelve petals representing the twelve signs of the Zodiac. Their colouring cannot easily be described as it consists of blended pastel shades. The letters of the Hebrew alphabet are attributed to these twenty-two petals and also to the twenty two Paths on the Tree of Life, and when the two symbols are used conjointly according to the traditional technique, they supply the key to the symbolism of the Mysteries.

This work is taught in our Inner Group, but those who find the Many-petalled Rose too intricate a symbol to use in private meditation may equally well make use of its simpler, mystical form. In group meditation the trained members of the group build the visual image, thus rendering it available for all who participate, whether trained or not. The Rose-cross acts as our key-call in the same way as the dialling of a telephone number.

Having formulated the Rose-cross, we next visualise it as standing in the centre of a cavern under the Hill of Vision. This cavern is a traditional meeting place on the astral plane. We rise to that level of consciousness when we visualise it, and those who come to us in the light descend to that level by the use of the same method. A few words concerning who and what they are may be helpful to those to whom the esoteric doctrines are unfamiliar.

It is held that initiates trained in the methods of the higher psychism pass out in full consciousness when they die, and are given the choice of entering their rest or of remaining in the earth-sphere and continuing their work. Many choose the latter course: of these are those who come to join us in the light; trained in the same methods as we are, and accustomed to employing the same symbolism, the use of the Rose-cross formula calls them up.

These things may be said now because the time for the drawing back of the veil upon a further grade of the Mysteries has come. During the last war, spiritualism, from being the more or less persecuted study of the few, won its place in the general thought of the times. In this war the same thing will happen with occultism, which is a deeper and more comprehensive aspect of the same subject.

To describe the technique, however, is not to reveal the secrets, any more than the writing of a book on violin playing. The higher psychism is an art in which knowledge must be combined with experience and based on natural aptitude if results are to be obtained. Nevertheless, under the new dispensation now beginning, all who will are entitled to try to use the key, but only for those who are found worthy will the lock turn.

15 June 1941 – In Moscow yesterday, in the wake of rumours of a German offensive, Foreign Minister Molotov said that "only a fool would attack Russia."

Letter seventy-seven draws attention to the wider horizon of the forthcoming ideals of the Aquarian Age, with Dion Fortune's view of how the current esoteric work is preparing for it.

LETTER 77
for June 15th 1941

The Piscean Age has passed and the Aquarian Age is drawing away from the phase that astrologers call the cusp, or sphere of mingled influences, and beginning to show its true characteristics. Not only are all the conditions of life changing, but its moral standards also. This does not mean that there will be no standards of conduct in the Aquarian Age and that freedom will be extended into anarchy; there are certain standards that are eternal, such as truth and honesty; but there are others that change with the changing age; for the qualities which make a man a good citizen in war time may make him a gangster in peace, and the qualities that make a man a good citizen in peace may make him a brake on the wheel in warfare. We must learn to read the lessons of history and profit by them. Different conditions make different demands, and the qualities that constitute good citizenship change with the changing times, though the fundamental standards abide.

The war is breaking up everything we have and are. Bombing is breaking up whole districts; evacuation is breaking up family ties. There is much talk and thought of reconstruction and re-building, but do we propose to rebuild as before on the vacant sites, having strict regard to the rights of ownership as was done after the Fire of London, when Sir Christopher Wren's great design was scrapped, or do we propose to build anew upon the eternal verities?

We have been given a formula expressed in symbolism which we call the Threefold Glyph. Through meditation on this glyph we shall perceive the basic principles applying to whatever problem we seek to solve. It is not for us to enter into the sphere of practical politics, but it is our task to discover the principles that are to guide the New Age that is dawning.

We can easily see that the symbol of King Arthur wielding Excalibur refers to Geburah and gives us the formula for dealing with actual evil, for defending our country against external foes, maintaining law and order in the face of civil crime and corruption, and dealing with personal problems wherein we have to assert our rights against oppression and aggression. That formula, the glyph teaches us, is chivalry, not pacifism.

The figure of the wise Merlin, seated in stability on his throne and holding the Diamond Sceptre and the Golden Orb, teaches us the formula of Gedulah or Chesed, social organisation in time of peace. This is a formula of power through knowledge, not physical force, and the orb represents the unity to which all things must be brought. The third figure in the Purple Ray, which is a bonding of the Red and the Blue, is that of a woman standing upon the globe of Earth rising from the Waters; her head crowned with the crescent moon and in her hands a cup. The blending of the Rays tells us that we are dealing with the factor of functional equilibrium, which, of course depends on the principle of polarity, and we may deduce that it concerns the right relationship of men and women in family life which is the basic unit upon which the state must be built.

Looking back on the age that is passing we see certain outstanding problems. We do not wish to carry these over into the New Age, and so re-infect our national life; therefore we must find a formula that will solve them. The first problem that we shall have to solve is economic, for all else hangs on that. Our economic troubles arise from two primary factors, ignorance and selfishness; the ignorance that does not realise what is wrong, and the selfishness that refuses to let go privileges in order that reorganisation may be effected. The cure for these troubles is education in its true sense, that is to say, education in wisdom, not merely education in knowledge. Wisdom consists of a threefold blend of knowledge, right moral principles, and practical commonsense.

> *22 June 1941 – Three million German troops attack the USSR along an 1800 mile front. Churchill promises to give Russia all possible help.*

The following letter again draws the important practical distinction between a group mind and a group soul in the destiny of nations.

LETTER 78
for June 22nd 1941

There is an important difference between group mind and the group soul. The group soul may be compared to the subconsciousness of the race, and the group mind to its collective consciousness. The group soul has been built up slowly during the passage of centuries; it is not easily changed or modified. The group mind changes swiftly and easily; it can be swayed by orators and journalists; it is, moreover, sectional, divided up according to social and sectional interests.

It is very important to study the action and interaction of the group mind and group soul. There is a point where they meet; when the group soul can gradually be changed by the cumulative influence of the group mind; and equally when energised by stress, the group soul can rise up and dominate the group mind, binding all its warring parts into unity.

The group soul, having been built up slowly during the long ages of history, is very stable and resistant; nevertheless, changes in the group mind influence it, given time. Note the great changes brought about by religious influence and education; the manner in which Merrie England grew dour during the Puritan regime; the manner in which the Restoration let loose grossness; the reaction brought about by the Evangelical influence in the Victorian age, and the reactions developing out of two world wars, and the developments of analytical psychology and its concept of human nature.

But throughout all this the basic characteristics of the race remain constant. The influence of the current phases of the group mind determines the mode of manifestation of these characteristics, but never totally eradicates them.

The influence of the group soul on the group mind is only felt in times of crisis. It is well represented by such legends as Drake's Drum and the Angels of Mons, and whether these are literally true or not, they are psychologically valid.

When a man is in danger, his primitive impulses take over control and direct his actions in proportion to the degree of organisation of his conscious mind. In people of undeveloped mentality, panic is easily induced, whereas the habit of discipline will hold fast even in the face of death by those inured to it.

Conscious and subconscious impulses are usually considered as being at perpetual cross-purposes, and so they are in people whose outlook on life is unreal or sophisticated; but in those in whom subconsciousness and consciousness are in harmony, wonderful resources are at the disposal of the rational self because the elemental forces of the deeper levels are made available.

It is the aim of both psychotherapy and initiation to bring about harmonisation between consciousness and subconsciousness. Both methods of dealing with the human mind depend for their results on the same factor – the resources made available to the personality when this unification takes place. Initiation differs from psychoanalysis in that it carries the process a stage further and unites subconsciousness with cosmic consciousness; save for this, the two methods have more in common than either of them realises.

21 September 1941 – The code-breaker, Enigma, gives Britain and the USSR advanced warning of a German all-out attack on Moscow.

There now enters a mood of confidence in the outcome of the war, and a looking forward to the challenges of peace.

LETTER 84
for September 21st 1941

The war need cause us no anxiety; it is already won on the Inner Planes, but we have a great and pressing need to take anxious thought for the peace lest we once again be defrauded of the fruits of our efforts. There will be an attempt made – an attempt already conceived and undergoing planning, to fob us off with the minimum of superficial social reform while retaining the status quo in all fundamental matters of economics and the ethics of human relationships. This is not good enough. The new wine of a New Age cannot be poured into the old bottles of outworn codes. There must be fundamental changes in the way of national life because a fundamental change is taking place in Life itself as the sun moves from Pisces to Aquarius in the precession of the Equinoxes. Let us not merely hope, but strive and pray that this takes place through evolution and not through revolution; for take place it will, and if not by one method, then by another. If we who have borne the burden and heat of the day are not to be defrauded of our just dues we must carry over into the peace the momentum of war – the willingness to make sacrifices and undergo discipline. How ironic it is that the money which could not be found for social reform was poured forth a hundred-fold for tanks and planes when the impact of the bombs roused us out of our complacency and selfishness, and how grim a comment on our national morale that it took high explosive to stir the national consciousness.

We must work for two things – the morale that will carry the momentum of war into the work of reconstruction, and the coming forth of the leaders who shall embody the new ideas. The men who should have led us lie in Flanders fields, but their death released energy, being sacrificial, and upon that energy we can draw for the reconstruction.

5 October 1941 – In their attack on Moscow, German losses are estimated at 3 million and Russian losses at 1.1 million.

This optimism is continued after the Autumnal Equinox of 1941 but there enters a sombre warning about subtler challenges yet to come, and particular instances in the way that occult forces may be used by hostile powers.

LETTER 86
for October 5th 1941

All the signs on the physical plane indicate that the war has rounded the turning point and is entering upon its penultimate phase, though it could still be thrown away by weakness and folly, of which we must take heed that we are not guilty.

A new danger will threaten us, however, as it becomes apparent that the military might of Germany has shot its bolt. There are two schools of thought in the entourage of the Fuehrer – those who believe in the invincibility of physical force and rely on mundane plan organisation to achieve their ends; and the relatively small and apparently obscure group of those who realise that there are subtle forces that can be enlisted to serve their ends. Hitler himself uses both as his instruments. It is difficult to see how far he has an accurate knowledge of technical occultism and how far, as in military matters, he avails himself of the services of experts. In any case, he himself is a natural occultist and highly developed medium. We should probably not be far from the mark if we said that he has a natural flair for occult matters but has been at no pains to master the laborious technicalities of magic and relies on others for the working out of the details. That he employs astrologers to work out the timing of his strokes is well established and a matter of common knowledge; but it is doubtful, knowing as much as he does, this is the only line of occultism along which he works.

In his book *Strange Conflict*, Dennis Wheatley deals with the possibility of the employment of telepathic mind-reading for the penetration of state secrets, and any student of the occult knows that such a thing is not only possible, but far from improbable. We ourselves received three days warning of the outbreak of hostilities. But telepathic suggestion is just as much a fact as telepathic mind-reading, and we should do well to consider the possibilities it presents and the means of defence against them, for as the physical plane might of Germany declines, so will the influence of its exponents; and the Fuehrer will turn increasingly to those who wield the invisible weapons, and they are quite capable of snatching victory out of defeat after the war has been lost on the physical plane. We might very well be robbed of the fruits of victory in the very hour of our triumph by the apparently unaccountable aberrations of our leaders, who would allow a Germany on the verge of breaking, but not actually broken, to slip through their fingers, retreat and re-arm. Then there would be another war in ten years' time, and we should not win it.

There is only one defence against such subtle methods working in darkness, and that is to dig them up and expose them to the light of the sun, for light destroys the creatures of darkness, being inimical to their nature. Suggestion, however subtle, is useless against the person who knows it is being employed. If the possibility is realised, people can be on their guard against it.

Is such a danger real or fantastic? Let me give an example. It will be recalled that shortly after the outbreak of war there was for several weeks an epidemic of thefts of important secret documents from attaché cases left in unattended cars. Then the epidemic ceased as suddenly as it had begun. For such an epidemic the following factors were necessary:

(i) The leaving of important documents in cars on a wholesale scale.

(ii) The presence on the spot on each occasion of a car thief interested in official secrets and capable of realising their value when he saw them, for the ordinary car thief pitches mere papers into the nearest bushes if he has the misfortune to steal them in mistake for "valuables".

How are we to explain such phenomenal absent-mindedness on the part of custodians of important papers, plus the presence on the spot of a specialist thief? Would not telepathic suggestion account for the happenings more satisfactorily than any other hypothesis?

How can not only those in high positions, but the individual voter who is an important person in a democracy, avoid being caught in this invisible snare? In one way only – the traditional magical manner – by swearing the Oath of the Operation.

This is done by defining the nature of the work undertaken and laying down its conditions in principle and in detail, and swearing a solemn oath not to depart one hair's breadth from them whatever may be the confusions and temptations. In our case the Oath of the Operation is the Atlantic Charter. Every man, woman, and child ranged on the side of the Free Nations against Hitler's New Order ought to acquaint themselves thoroughly with the terms of that agreement and the nature of the principles involved, and resolve in their hearts that in no circumstances and for no considerations whatever will they swerve from them by a hair's breadth. Let them realise that the subtlest and the most forcible temptations to compromise will come to them, not only in the form of considerations of expediency and threats, but disguised as ideals, the voice of conscience, the promptings of mercy, and even psychic intuitions – in fact especially the latter. Compromise will be "in the air" as soon as the military defeat of Germany is a certainty. There is only one defence against the potent invisible influences that will then commence coming over on the aether in concentrated form – the strict, blind, even fanatical observance of the Oath of the Operation – for when that intangible bombardment begins, we shall be too bemused to be capable of judgement.

> *12 October 1941 – This week mud and rain slows down the German advance towards Moscow. By now, German forces are within 60 miles of the Russian capital.*

The deep and sinister matters of the previous letter are pursued in the one that follows, and Dion Fortune goes on, in the very explicit terms, to describe how such dangers may be guarded against.

LETTER 87
for October 12th 1941

Those who have read last week's letter will no doubt have realised from incidents within their own observation the truth it indicates. We have only to look backwards over the record of British policy during and immediately preceding the war to realise that some abnormal influence was at work, for human fatuity could hardly have touched such depths unaided. No one suggests, nor I think, would anyone believe, that English statesmen and diplomats were "got at" through the commonplace channels of corruption; what then was the nature of the influence that undermined their judgement? For this war ought never to have occurred, and need never have occurred if a normal standard of commonsense had prevailed in high places. How did it come about that a man of the calibre of "Mr Schickelgruber", presiding over a state with a record like Germany's, could mislead men of the calibre of the leaders of the British people?

The power of democratic leadership is not found in insensitive persons with insulated minds, and the awareness of subtle influences which makes them able to discern the signs of the times renders them vulnerable to the impact of forces deliberately transmitted over that subtle mental radio which can be operated by trained minds. It is no use stigmatising such an operation as black magic, for this mental radio is as impersonal as Marconi's invention. It is this power that we ourselves make use of in our group meditations week by week, but we endeavour to use it in humility and dedication and self-examination, for no personal or national end, but for the good of all living beings, working for national purposes because we believe the group soul of the British people to be dedicated to the service of God insofar as the group mind can conceive it.

It is our task, being students of the Secret Wisdom, to use the knowledge our studies have yielded us to aid in the carrying out of the Cosmic Law, humbly before God, but with the courage of our convictions before our fellow men. There are methods known in the Secret Tradition which can be used, and it is our task to use them.

We too can evoke primordial energies from the primitive levels of the national group soul and harness them to archetypal ideas in the group mind of the race. Let us consider the method to be employed.

When the Germans open up the primordial levels of their racial mind they release the elemental energies of the old gods – the bloodstained, mindless images of the heroes of Norse myth. Do we necessarily fight them with their own weapons? Far otherwise. The Kelts of these islands were among the earliest to be Christianised, as the Germans were among the latest. A good thousand years intervenes between the conversion of Britain and the conversion of Germany; consequently the influences of Christianity reaches to a far deeper level of racial consciousness with us than with them, and when the surface consciousness of the British group soul peels off we find, not the mindless heroes of Valhalla, but the chivalry of the Table Round; Excalibur instead of Nothung, and the Quest of the Grail instead of the looting of the Rhinegold.

Let us wake from their long sleep the primordial images of our race, King Arthur and his knights, with the wisdom of Merlin to guide them. These shall keep the soul of England against the invisible influences being brought to bear upon it for its undoing. Let the folly of the pre-war years, during which the soul of England lay in a drugged sleep, give place to the ideal of chivalry. We know now what the drug was, and how the drugging was done. We need not fall victim again.

Let an ideal, clearly held, guard the soul of England against insidious propaganda. Let the archetypal images of the Age of Faith arise to guide us, and the primordial energies of our ancient race be loosed on a Quest.

2 November 1941 – This week the Germans stop their land attack on Moscow to wait for the ground to harden. Meanwhile the Luftwaffe relentlessly bomb the city.

In her ninetieth letter Dion Fortune extends the question of self protection from the nation to the individual. This instruction is probably as valuable as anything she wrote in her earlier popular book *Psychic Self-Defence*.

LETTER 90
for November 2nd 1941

We have recently pointed out in plain terms that the knowledge of mind power can be used for attack as well as defence, and that our enemies are well known to have access to the occult methods. Occultism is neither foolproof nor knave-proof; it is simply knowledge of certain little-understood aspects of the human mind, and can be used for good or evil according to the motives that inspire it. Our own methods can be turned against us unless we understand the use of the shield as well as the sword. It has been suggested that in attacking our antagonists openly as we have done, we render ourselves liable to a deliberate riposte; this is a suggestion that cannot be brushed aside with platitudes, but must be taken seriously. Of course we can be attacked, and if we are accomplishing anything effectual, an attack will certainly be made. What is the best defence against such an attack? For the faint-hearted, the best defence is to drop all contact with the Fraternity of the Inner Light, and run away removing their precious skins to a place of safety, if they can find one. This is the best thing for them, and the best thing for us, for there is no efficient defence for the faint-hearted in these matters.

There is, however, a perfectly efficient defence for the courageous and dedicated. Just as the skin, if unbroken, offers a strong defence against contagion, so the surface of the aura is as resistant as plate glass when hardened for defence, for the citadel of the soul can only be betrayed from within. If we react to an attack, we open the gates; if we do not react, the forces sent against us recoil from the glassy surface of the aura and return to those that sent them like an A.A. shell that has failed to explode.

The best way to stiffen the resistive surface of the aura is to raise the magnetic pressure inside. This is done by invocation. Realise that in using our knowledge of mind power in the fight for what we believe to be right, we are not relying on our own recourses, but making channels of ourselves for spiritual forces coming down from a higher plan and directed by a higher wisdom. We are neither going in our own strength nor acting on our own judgement, but have dedicated ourselves to the service of the One Good, which is God, even to the point of the final sacrifice. It is not our personal activities that stir up opposition and invite retaliation; it is the forces of Cosmic Law that are using us as channels, and these are fully able to protect the channels they are using from any attack that can be made upon them. Realising this, we shall see that there is no occasion to feel fear, we are invulnerable to a frontal attack.

Before and after meditation, and on going to bed at night, we should remind ourselves of this protection. If there should be any definite sense of attack, imagine yourself standing before the Rose-Cross in the Cavern under the Hill of Vision; see the doors opening and the Ray of Light shining in, and Those entering, who come to meet us in the Light. Imagine yourself speaking to Them; tell Them what you feel, and ask for Their protection. We should be interested to know if anyone has occasion to use this method, and the results they get.

There are possibilities of flank attacks, however, to which we need to be alive. The fear-inspiring threat of indiscriminate bombing has been tried, and has failed. Despite its physical effects it was purely psychological warfare, for its effect on our war effort was negligible. We need now to begin our preparations to meet what will surely come – the flank attacks on morale, the familiar pincer movement repeated on the Inner Planes.

These attacks rely on the principle that good is the enemy of the best. It would be good to stop the war at once, but it would be better to make sure of a permanent peace by fighting it to a conclusive finish. Since we have shown ourselves so notably unresponsive to psychological warfare based on terrorist principles, an appeal to our notoriously sentimental idealism will be attempted.

In combating this, we shall need great wisdom, for there is a true idealism of which we must not lose sight while refusing to allow the wool to be pulled over our eyes by specious statements of false idealism. In this matter the principle of justice is our best guide. There can be no compromise on this point, especially where other people's rights are concerned.

I should like to take this opportunity of assuring our friends that the rumour that I am suffering from a general breakdown brought on by the intensity of my Inner Plane activities in the defence of England does not correctly describe the situation. The trouble is not generalised, but localised in my nose, and the symptoms are those of the common cold. While I would be willing to believe anything of Hitler in the way of frightfulness, I think that in this instance he should be given the benefit of the doubt and the trouble attributed to natural causes.

I do not know of anything that could have given rise to this rumour, but in the light of the matters we have concerned in this Letter, I conclude that the wish was father to the thought.

7 December 1941 – Suffering in conditions so cold that their weapons seize, the German army is dramatically pushed back by a secretly gathered army of Russians. The Germans had been within 12 miles of the Kremlin.

Towards the end of 1941 Dion Fortune announced the re-establishment of the inner aspects of her work, which meant less participation by her in elementary teaching activity. In her description of the work in hand she again gives an excellent cameo of the work of a dedicated occult group.

LETTER 95
for December 7th 1941

A great deal of reorganisation is going on in our work, necessitating my partial withdrawal from Outer Court activities, and I feel that some explanation is due to the friends who have been attending my lectures on Sunday mornings. Although we had to restrict our activities owing to the black-out and the dispersal of our workers, we carried on right through the blitz by temporarily combining our Inner and Outer Court, so that those who come to the open meetings on Sundays were invited to participate in Inner Group meditation work. We are, however, essentially an organisation for intensive training, not for propaganda work, and with the return of less strenuous conditions we are resuming our original functions. As always, our study courses are open to all serious students, but we shall not be doing the deeper work or giving the deeper teaching in the public lectures of the Outer Court any longer. Meanwhile, those who have learnt our meditation methods are asked to carry on as heretofore with the weekly work.

I have already said, our work as an organisation has been the intensive training of advanced students and we have had no contact with the general public, those who came to us coming either as a result of reading my books or through personal introduction. In order to give the advanced training, however, it was necessary to recover a great many of the Lost Secrets of the Mystery Tradition, for so many had been lost that the system was for all practical purposes inoperative and largely unintelligible. In order to carry out this work I have only sought for a sufficient number of students of a suitable type to assist me with the research work, and never made any attempt to draw large numbers around me, propaganda not being my work. Sufficient students of the right type, however, have never been easy to find, even among the most enthusiastic, and there have been many disappointments on both sides. This, I hope, involves no odium. It certainly does not on our side, for people may do good work with other organisations who are unsuited to ours. Unfortunately there have been from time to time people who have found it hard to forgive us our exacting standard. I would point out, however, that if we are to have anything worth giving to worthwhile people, we must exact a high standard and that an organisation doing practical work cannot afford to carry more than a very limited amount of dead weight in the form of "passengers", who, however sincerely interested they may be, either cannot make, or do not desire to fulfil the conditions requisite for making any active psychic contribution to our work.

Up to the outbreak of the war we were occupied with gathering the battered remains of the Mystery Tradition, piecing them together, and interpreting them to modern thought in terms of psychology. The basis of this work rested on the papers left behind by the late MacGregor Mathers, founder of the Hermetic Order of the Golden Dawn, a complete set of which are in my possession, though I had not got permission to publish them. They were, however, subsequently published by Israel Regardie in four volumes under the title of *The Golden Dawn.* Those who have had access to these very valuable volumes will realise how much work was necessary to reconstruct the lost verbal tradition and provide the necessary practical experience to enable the practical work to be carried out effectually and make of it a reality instead of a vain observance. It will be many a long day, and require the co-operation of many persons with highly specialised qualifications, before this work can be considered complete, if it ever is, for fresh vistas open as one advances – but substantial progress has been made, and is in process of making, and in the fruits of this and in further research we invite the co-operation of those who are willing to work at the matter systematically and seriously. I shall not, however, in future, be speaking in public oftener than once a month, though the Sunday morning lectures will continue with other speakers; particulars of the programme for next term will be sent in due course to all those whose addresses we have. During the blackout our activities must necessarily be limited, but as the days grow longer in the spring they will be again extended.

The research work, and the work of building up a Mystery School and method of systematic training, will continue as heretofore; and we shall also continue our meditation work in support of the aims set forth in the Atlantic Charter. In this all who will can aid, whether they be members of our organisation or not, and these Letters will continue to be sent out weekly in order to co-ordinate their efforts.

14 December 1941 – Six days ago Japan attacked the American Pacific Fleet at Pearl Harbor in the Hawaiian Islands.

By the time of writing her ninety-sixth letter, the war had extended yet further, with the coming in of Japan and war in the Pacific. In taking note of this, Dion Fortune makes some useful observations about the difference between psychism and seership, and their relation to the foreseeing of coming events.

LETTER 96
for December 14th 1941

Since our last letter was written and despatched the picture presented by the war has changed notably; it has now spread right round the globe and can justly be termed a World War and not a European War, a title which has hitherto been withheld from it despite the wise words that peace is one and indivisible.

This new development brings to the forefront the question of prophecy, which is often raised in connection with the teachings received from the Inner Planes. Why do not the Masters, if they are what they are presumed to be, exercise the power of prophecy for the benefit of humanity? The answer is that they do, but they seldom set time limits for the working out of their prognostications, so that although the esoteric teachings afford valuable information for the planning of strategy, they give little help in the devising of tactics. In other words, the teaching received from the Masters is a guide to long distance planning, but leaves immediate problems to the exercise of judgement and initiative on the physical plane. It would be difficult to conceive a wiser policy, for it gives guidance in questions of principle without which men must stumble blindly, and leaves us to benefit by the exercise of responsibility.

It will be remembered that throughout the dubious developments of 1939 and the dark experiences of 1941, the tone of these letters never varied; the question of the ultimate outcome of the war and the form of the final peace was never considered a matter for speculation because it was taken for granted. Well informed persons shrugged their shoulders, but time is justifying that attitude. It is a curious fact that all the pessimism was in high places; the mass of the people of Britain, relying on instinct instead of information, took the same view that we, guided by seership, were led to take. Exact information can be very misleading because it only takes account of what is already in manifestation on the physical plane, and makes no allowance for imponderable psychological factors and the subtle forces of the Inner Planes, which are the planes of causation, where all things brew before they come through to the physical plane. The psychic looks beyond the realms of material manifestation and sees the shape of things to come a little while before they manifest; consequently he can make exact prophecies if he is able to assess the relative influence of the various factors involved.

The seer, however, works differently. His vision operates on the plane of remote causation and he sees primary causes at work; in consequence he can foretell the end result of tendencies as they work out in the epochs of history but has little guidance to offer on the day to day movements of events.

21 December 1941 – President Roosevelt is given extraordinary war powers by Congress and lowers the minimum age for military service to 19.

The role of a working group is reiterated in the following letter and the importance of its contact with the Masters or Elder Brethren upon the Inner Planes.

LETTER 97
for December 21st 1941

The work which we are engaged in doing in our meditation group is not a rule of thumb affair; it is based on the profound philosophic principles of the esoteric tradition. It is not possible in these letters to make a study for these principles in their entirety, but enough must be said for the rationale of our work to be understood so that those who are taking part can co-operate intelligently and use the powers made available for us to the best advantage.

We conceive of God as the Great Unmanifest and therefore transcending human realisation and only to be known by deduction from His manifestation in the Cosmos, which we conceive as a projected thought form of the Divine Mind. We conceive of sparks from the Divine Fire which is the Great Unmanifest as forming the nuclei of the souls of men. These nuclei build up individual consciousness through the experiences of independent existence in manifestation. They develop up to a certain point under the complete control of cosmic law, such law having been built up in the course of previous evolutions; but after a certain point they have to go forward under their own guidance and power in order to achieve the higher ranges of development open to them as the sons of God, that is to say, as sparks from the Divine Fire, and therefore of the same nature as the Great Unmanifest. It is here that evil, or unbalanced force, enters in, for just as the child crawling about the floor and learning to walk is at a disadvantage as compared with the child lying safely in the comfort of the cradle, so the infant humanity progressing painfully towards self-conscious, self-controlled adulthood is at a disadvantage as compared with the mindless spiritual beings of the Golden Age. Nevertheless, without this painful phase of learning by experience mankind could never achieve spiritual adulthood and responsibility. We know only too well the kind of personality that results when an adolescent is denied all opportunity for experience and treated as a child by unwise parents; there is also a form of insanity which consists in the refusal to face life and a return to the infantile attitude. Both these things we see in the life of nations as well as individuals, and they help to explain what is happening in the world today.

We know that children are not left to learn by their own unaided experience, but that adults take on the task of teaching them the cultural heritage of the race. This takes place also on group level. There are teachers of mankind, handing on the accumulated experience of previous evolutions, and these we call the Masters or Elder Brethren. They are of human, not the angelic evolution, and are disembodied minds existing on the Inner Planes. They guide and teach by projecting thought telepathically, relaying the archetypal ideas of the Divine Mind. People who are sensitive to spiritual influences receive these ideas subconsciously and begin to act upon them without realising whence they come; they receive them as general principles, however, not as concrete direction of policy. People with psychic development perceive these influences more clearly, according to their degree of development; the highly trained initiates of the occult schools are in direct and conscious touch with the Masters. Thus is it possible for humanity to receive guidance in so far as it is capable of profiting by such guidance, and it is not left to grope unaided. Our work as a group consists in maintaining contact with the Masters on the Inner Planes so that this guidance and teaching can come through. In order to do this, we have to maintain certain conditions at our headquarters, and this demands the services of a certain number of carefully chosen and highly trained people. In order to discover and develop such servers we maintain an Outer Court and training school.

25 January 1942 – The first American troops arrive on British soil.

I have heard it said that Dion Fortune, in her social attitudes, was something of a snob. This would hardly seem to be supported by her trenchant remarks about social privilege in her hundredth letter. She also gives some hard practical advice on how to help remedy things – although not by going to the barricades!

LETTER 100
for January 25th 1942

We are far from being a voice crying in the wilderness when we proclaim the mental deadness, and even decomposition, of the ruling classes of this country; the classes that supply the personnel of the higher grades of the Services, that conduct our foreign diplomacy, direct our Colonial Empire and staff our Civil Service, for it is hardly possible to rise to the senior posts unless one derives from the proper circles because those who make the appointments consider not only the professional qualifications of the applicant, but also his social ones. Will he be a pleasant person to work with, or a disturber of ancient peace? Is his wife socially acceptable to their wives? Incidentally it may be noted that the most efficient persons are seldom particularly pleasant to work with and that petticoat influence is one sign of corruption. One may say, with little risk of contradiction, that driving force, originality, enterprise and a willingness to take risks and responsibility are in inverse ratio to seniority, for a man with those qualities is a nuisance to his seniors, who will not admit him to their midst if the choice lies with them, which is very understandable, for old dogs do not like learning new tricks, and changes might result from the introduction of originality and courage.

The record of the fighting in the present war shows that our tactics are good, but our strategy deplorable. "Lions led by donkeys" is as true a comment on our nation today as it was when it was uttered a hundred and fifty years ago.

If all this be so, and everyone except the persons concerned seem to think it is, what can we, working in a meditating circle, do about it? It can readily be seen that, if telepathy is fact, we can affect national morale, but can we exert any influence on the efficiency of high places and high placemen? Yes, we can, and by the old, traditional method of sympathetic magic. The primitive man, when he wishes it to rain, invokes the rain god and sprinkles water. Algernon Blackwood in his fascinating short story "The Regeneration of Lord Ernie", in *Incredible Adventures*, tells of the fire dance in which the participants imitate the leaping of the flames and so fill themselves with fiery energy.

As has often been pointed out in these Letters, we can help to bring in the Aquarian Age by living individually in the Aquarian manner. Even those who do not understand occultism can understand the power of example; but there is another factor in the matter as well as example. The sprinkling of water alone is not sufficient to induce the rain to fall – the rain god has to be invoked, just as it is not enough merely to receive the Eucharist passively, it has to be received "with intention". If we live in the Aquarian way "with intention" we shall exercise more power than that of example as has so often been said before in these Letters; we shall inoculate the group mind of the race at the subconscious level.

We can influence the efficiency of our government by deliberately practising 'with intention' in our own lives the qualities we wish to see expressed in the national life. Are we disgusted with complacency? Then let us cease to be complacent for the sake of peace and quietness with our relatives, our employees and our employers. Let us have a little private blitzkrieg of our own in the home circle, rooting out long-standing abuses, doing it ritualistically, "with incantation", identifying ourselves with the group soul of the race, and we shall soon see things beginning to happen in high places.

8 February 1942 – Following the death of Fritz Todt, Hitler makes Albert Speer armaments minister.

Dion Fortune returns to the theme of how to improve the world by esoteric endeavour in the next letter but one. And it might be remembered that the principles and methods she enunciated then, can apply and be would be worked equally validly now.

LETTER 102
for February 8th 1942

The New Age demands a new spirit, and it is pretty clear by now that the new spirit is not going to come in from the top; it is going to rise up from the depths of the racial subconsciousness. How can those who do not occupy a position of influence play their part in bringing in the New Age? Leaderless, unorganised, with no means of making their influence felt in the face of vested interests and well-organised political machinery, what can they do that can in any way influence the course of events?

Upon the physical plane they can do little or nothing, but in the kingdom of the Unseen they can exercise a potent influence if they make use of that knowledge which is power – the ancient, secret wisdom of the Mystics. There are two ways in which this power is exercised, and the one is ineffectual without the other. Both ways are well known, and there is no secret about them; the secret lies in the knowledge of the power that is brought to bear by their combination.

First of all, let each one of us try to discern, through study, observation and meditation, the lines along which the ideals of the New Age are shaping. Ignoring the grim spectre of actuality and practicality, which, viewed from the physical plane, looms like a death's head, let them discern the ideal archetypes upon the Inner Planes that are already overshadowing this warring earth, struggling in the birth throes, even as the soul of the unborn child overshadows a pregnant woman. Only great seers can perceive the vision in its fullness, but all men of good will can catch some glimmer of it, and in so far as they see that light can live by it if they have the necessary courage, for it requires courage to defy custom and prejudice and walk in the light of a day that has not yet dawned.

It will be necessary to face difficulties and make sacrifices, and there will be martyrs. Individuals must dare to live in the light they have discerned by means of the inner vision before it has come through to the physical plane; by so doing, they themselves actually bring it through to the physical plane and it is then in manifestation, and what is in manifestation can no more be thrust into limbo again than the chick be put back into the egg. There it is, and it has to be reckoned with, for it has taken its place in the group consciousness and will work like yeast. If it is not along the lines of evolving life, the tide of life, setting against it, will neutralize it.

Power is necessary, however, in order to exert this subtle but effectual influence, for no lever can work of itself. How then, you will ask, can the uninfluential exercise power? They can exercise the power that is set free by sacrifice. If they are prepared to suffer for their ideals. If each man and woman who sees the vision of the New Age will live in that light in the face of ridicule and resistance and penalisation, defying the pressure of public opinion and the organised forces of convention, they will suffer for their opinions; but if they persevere while suffering, the pain and distress they undergo thus voluntarily can be dedicated to the service of mankind; it will then exert pressure on that great lever whose fulcrum is not on this plane and which can move mountains.

This is the secret of power – discern the course of things to come; shape your own life accordingly; lay upon the altar of sacrifice the suffering that will be your lot, and you can move the world. That is the way in which all reforms have been brought about, and it will always bring about reform if persevered in with sufficient determination, for neither principalities nor powers can prevail against the leverage derived from a fulcrum on the spiritual plane. But never forget that a lever cannot act of itself; spiritual power will not bring about material things unless sacrifice sets it in motion.

> *29 March 1942 – Using the new "Gee" navigation system, RAF bombers devastate the German port of Lubeck. Over 30% of the town is destroyed.*

The principle of sacrifice as a means of power is again emphasised in the one hundred and ninth letter, with a practical example from the group itself. There is also food for thought in the talismanic power there can be in writing a letter of protest with spiritual intention.

LETTER 109
for March 29th 1942

Spiritual powers only take effect on the physical plane when they are translated into action: this is the significance and raison d'être of ritual. Two things are necessary for the bringing through of magical power into manifestation – some form of action and some form of sacrifice. The action may be symbolic and the sacrifice no more than a risk, but nevertheless both these things must be done and incurred. If we had evacuated to Glastonbury, as we very well could have done, when the Battle of London began to get hot, we should not have been able to put into those Letters the power that people have felt in them. Equally, it is not enough for us to point out the spiritual principles involved in reconstruction if we are not prepared to call down on ourselves the wrath of the Powers that Be if we see those principles put in jeopardy. Individuals can likewise make their powers felt by writing letters to their local papers and their Members of Parliament. More is effected in this way than is generally realised. If every individual dares to be "A voice crying in the wilderness" there arises a clamour that makes itself heard even above the voice of the guns.

How, it may be asked, can the unarmed prevail against the armed in matter of oppression? There is one way in which he can always prevail – he can stand up in the name of spiritual principle and say: Shoot and be damned! And if the armed man shoot, he is damned. History bears witness to this fact on every page.

---

26 April 1942 – In Berlin, Adolf Hitler takes absolute power in Germany. All laws that might stand in his way are abolished.

In the one hundred and thirteenth letter Dion Fortune begins to look forward to the reconstruction of the shattered world when the war is over. Her firm view is that things are never going to be quite the same as once they were. Again she comments upon the synchronicities between the meditation work of the group since the early days of the war, and the ideas expressed in the leading forums of public opinion in the nation.

LETTER 113
for April 26th 1942

After the last war, despite all promises to the men who won it, the past was rebuilt on the original foundations by those in possession of power. This cannot happen again, for the basis on which that power rested – the control of the raw materials of the Empire – is being destroyed on such a large scale that only planned reconstruction can replace it. The spirit of the age will never allow the control of the bases of life to be exploited for private interest again. Private individuals cannot rebuild what has been destroyed, either in this country or overseas; only the nation as a whole can rebuild it, and what the nation builds, the nation owns.

What has been will never be again. The old security is gone, but new opportunity awaits us. Those who cannot adapt themselves to the new conditions will suffer, but those who can will find fullness of life. Study the characteristics of Aquarius in order to learn how the new order will shape itself. Aquarius is the breaker of barriers, the disturber, the bringer of new influences and impulses. Those who are set in their ways suffer at the hands of Aquarius. Those who are fluidic and dynamic rejoice in the fulfilment of their destiny. Life values, not money values, will set the new standards, and there will be a drastic revision of the rights of ownership...

As a matter of fact, the period of reconstruction has begun already. Those archetypal ideas we meditated upon in their primary form as spiritual ideals during the dark hours of the blitz have now taken intellectual form in the minds of the nation's thinkers, and experts are coming forward to formulate them to practical ends. It will be recalled that this was forecast in the earliest of these letters. The expression of the ideas then given archetypal form is finding an unexpected forum in the pages of *The Times*. Canterbury Cathedral and Printinghouse Square are the two last places where they might have been expected to make their appearance. We had faith in the promise made to us by the Masters, that these things we were meditating upon in Obscurity would be broadcast from the high places; but even our faith, which has had much to sustain it, did not run to this! One of two things is certain – either the Masters who gave the promise are what they claim to be, or the Warden of the Fraternity of the Inner Light is entitled to rank as a prophet alongside of Baalam's Ass, a position not without distinction. Anyway, somebody discerned the shape of things to come correctly. If it is my subconscious mind, I can only say that it is a very useful possession. It bid us hold steady during each false alarm. It warned us in time when the real crisis came: and it had alternative premises ready for us to move into when our headquarters were bombed. It also informed us that the cause of damage would be a time bomb, that the parts of our headquarters used for our work would not be seriously affected, and that there would be no casualties. The statue of the Master of Masters over the altar in the Sanctuary, which was moved over the edge of its plinth and turned half round by the shock of the explosion, stood as a silent witness amid the debris to Something which was not of this world.

If, however, we are right in our belief that spiritual influences govern the world, that these influences are not blind forces, but are transmitted intelligently through spiritual beings, and that those of humanity who are prepared to pay the price of selflessness may learn how to co-operate with Them, then we have great hope in our hearts and great possibilities in our hands.

> *10 May 1942 – Since it opened in March, 30,000 Jews from Lublin have died in the Belzec death camp in Poland.*

The one hundred and fifteenth letter presses home the theme of postwar reconstruction and the destiny and responsibility of all the nations, together with the role of individuals in the New Age. Ideals, we might say, that in many respects are still a long time coming, for a long list could be compiled of post-war atrocities, even to this day.

LETTER 115
for May 10th 1942

As soon as the bugles sound the "Cease Fire", there is only one practical thing to do – draw a line between past and present, and write the past off as a bad debt. If there had not been faults on both sides things would never have reached the pitch they did. There is little to choose on moral grounds between gangster methods and the moral inertia which allowed them to continue uninterfered with so long as they were applied to other people. If the Axis Powers have ill-treated their victims, do not let us forget that what are now the United Nations stood aside and allowed them to do so as long as they dared. It was only when we woke up to the danger ourselves that we took up arms; as long as questions of international morality and justice were at stake, we practised non-intervention and appeasement. Do not let us, if we value our self-respect, invite the opinion of either Spain or China on our record. We, as well as Germany, should be grateful to have the past forgotten. As far as the present is concerned, the calculated cruelties of Germany and Japan are matched by the sufferings caused through the ineptitude of England. The less said the better about moral responsibility for the sufferings of the world, for there is not one nation which can show a clean pair of hands in the cold light of history.

One thing can be safely prophesied when all else is uncertain – peace will dawn on a disorganised world. Nothing that was will remain and none will be immune. There will be no question of reconstruction, even if anyone desires to perpetuate the past, and it is difficult to believe that any save a favoured few would do so.

First and foremost, we must regard the planet of earth as a unit, in which no segregation is possible, owing to the development of communications, especially air-borne and ether-borne communications, and the interdependence of commerce all the world over. That peace is one and indivisible has been so amply demonstrated that it has become a truism; we must never lose sight of this fact again. Our planet of earth, and the human society thereon, must be organised as a whole, and if the democratic principle of government by consent of the governed means anything, it must be organised by a conference of victors as well as vanquished, together with the neutrals, if there are any neutrals left by that time. We must learn to stand back, as the Adept stands back, and view matters impersonally, on a basis of abstract justice, considering neither our own worthiness nor the moral turpitude of others, but simply human needs and the available means of meeting them, and the right attitude to be adopted in dealing with them. There are going to be starving people, diseased people and dangerous people in all the countries of the world. There are also going to be people whose spirits are open to the influx of the light of the new era. It is these people all over the earth who must make common cause if human society is to be saved. We cannot maintain spiritual and social lazar-houses and hope to escape the spread of infection from their sinister confines.

Nations must not be looked upon, nor think of themselves, as self-contained units; they are simply sub-sections of human society thus divided up for convenience of organisation. Co-ordination between the sub-sections is essential if the life of the planet earth is to be organised on any other than a predatory basis. The only basis for co-ordination is a spirit of mutual goodwill. Goodwill breeds goodwill, and someone has to make a start in this seething mass of human misunderstanding and misery. No nation can do it in the first instance, because the mass mind always functions at a lower level than the minds of individuals. It is the men and women of the New Age in all nations who must make contact across the national barriers as soon as the fighting is over, and they must meet as Aquarians, not as English, French or Germans. They must bring in the New Age for all men, not for their own people only, because the New Age is an age of co-ordination of the whole earth, and it cannot be brought in piecemeal. Those who share our ideals are on our side, whatever language they speak, whatever may be the colour of their skins or the shape of their skulls, or by whatever name they may call their God or gods, or no-gods.

> *31 May 1942 – The RAF launch the first ever 1000-bomber raid on Cologne. 1455 tons of bombs devastate the city. The raid is codenamed "Operation Millennium".*

Dion Fortune's remarks about the need for social changes sparked a reaction from some of her readers. She therefore felt it necessary to outline the principles upon which she, the Fraternity, and for that matter the Archbishop of Canterbury, stood.

LETTER 118
for May 31st 1942

A correspondent has raised the question of the political tone of these letters, so it may be as well to clarify the position. Our attitude is precisely that so well expressed by the new Archbishop of Canterbury in his book *Christianity and Social Order* issued in the Penguin series, to which we would ask our readers to refer for the detailed arguments and historical data whereby he defines the proper sphere of religious influence in social and political matters. Briefly, his contention is that religious organisations have the duty of guiding men's own minds concerning moral principles in social, economic and political matters, and of pronouncing a condemnation on whatever transgresses these: they should not, however, enter the arena of practical organisation nor take sides in party politics.

As these principles had been clearly in my mind for many long years before I read the Archbishop's book, wherein I found them confirmed with all the weight of scholarship and tradition, I trust I have never transgressed them in writing these letters.

Speaking as an initiate, from knowledge based both on tradition and on my own seership, I have stated that the old order has passed away, and a new phase of evolution is already with us. That it is the Age of Aquarius is an astronomical fact, calculated mathematically. Basing my conclusions on the occult teaching concerning the nature of Aquarius, I have tried to indicate how the New Age may be expected to work out. When I say the old forms of social organisation will break up, and everything will be in a state of flux, that racial and social barriers will be eroded and a general intermingling take place, I am not enunciating socialistic doctrines but astrological ones.

There will always be political parties – save in such circumstances that one successfully 'liquidates' the other – the Haves, who are content with the state of affairs and wish to preserve them, and the Have Nots, who are discontented with the state of affairs and wish to change them. Whether the Haves call themselves Conservatives, Unionists, or supporters of a National Government, or whether the Have Nots call themselves Radicals, Socialists or Communists, makes no difference – it is the viewpoint that counts. It has been said that political parties consist of the Outs and the Ins. When the Outs first get in they prove themselves Radicals, and when they have been in some time, they become Conservatives.

The Fraternity of the Inner Light, in its teaching concerning politics, enunciates principles based on Cosmic Law. It will be found that sometimes one, and sometimes another, and sometimes neither political party is moving along the line of these principles. We affirm the principle, but we do not say that this or that party is the exponent of them, for politics depend much more on personalities than on doctrines…

We say therefore to those who read these letters: Here are the cosmic principles; here are the basic factors of the problems that confront us as a society; sometimes one political party will be the most satisfactory at the moment, and sometimes the other; it is for you to decide which it is at the moment, it will be the other one presently, for that is the Law of the Cyclic Spiral. If this is to be called political bias, I can only say that it possesses the elasticity and ability to bend round curves of any material which is out on the bias, and can give little sense of security to the party it is supposed to support.

7 June 1942 – In retaliation for the assassination of Reinhardt Heydrich, Reich Protector of Bohemia, the Czech village of Lidice is razed to the ground and its population shot or deported.

In the letter following Dion Fortune reviews the record of inter-relationship that has been shown between the work of the group and the morale and ideas of the nation.

LETTER 119
for June 7th 1942

In last week's letter we pointed out that our teaching concerned principles, not politics. If those who have the back numbers of these letters will refer to them, they will see that these principles are today being expressed in politics. This is the way in which, as initiates, we work. We outline nothing; we meditate upon cosmic principles till these take intellectual form. If we are mistaken in our delineation, the formulation will be hazy and contradictory. If we have embodied it correctly, it will be clear-cut and coherent.

It may be said that in so acting we have actually done what we declared we had no intention of doing; but it will be seen that the delineation arises out of the meditation, and does not precede it. We do not set out with a clearly formed plan and meditate upon it; we set out with an abstract ideal based upon spiritual principle and out of it a concrete concept clarifies itself.

Now here comes the difference between participation in politics and the proper work of the servers of the mystical tradition of the race – having arrived at an intellectual clarification, we then stop, we do not meditate upon that concept, once having arrived at it; we take no steps to put it into practice or even to proselytise on its behalf. These letters circulate only among those who desire to participate in the meditation work. There is, in consequence, a gap between the initiates who bring through the archetypal ideas and the statesmen and economists who give them practical form. This gap forms the safety zone which prevents any wrong ideal or incorrectly formulated idea from being transmitted to the group mind of the race. The thought-forms that have developed as a result of group meditation work have to cross that gap by means of their own inherent energy. Unless the cosmic power is behind them, they will lack that energy. Unless they are in line with the spiritual ideals of the group mind they will be destroyed as they enter it in the same way as germs are destroyed as they enter the blood stream by the mobilised forces of the white blood corpuscles. The subconscious instincts of men detect and reject ideas that are alien to the radical ideals. Note how the attempts to instil hate and blood lust into the Anglo-Saxon soul have fallen to the ground. They are alien to our national temperament, and return like Noah's raven to him who sent them forth, having found no foothold. They have been destroyed by a spontaneous sense of disgust and – not to put too fine a point upon it – an innate sense of the ridiculous, which passes a judgement against which there is no appeal. The attempt to work up a hearty hate against Germany as a means of energising the war effort is rejected by a people fundamentally conditioned by Christianity and common sense.

Such efforts as these, though sincerely well-intentioned, are miscalculated. They are not in accordance with cosmic law and therefore prove abortive. They are destroyed, not so much by active opposition, as by the stolid unresponsiveness of the group mind to that which is out of alignment with its nature. On the other hand, these ideals to whose service we have dedicated ourselves are being given organic form by experts without any intervention on our part.

But as the things we have worked for are coming about without our active intervention, it may be said that they would have come about anyway, and all our work has been a waste of energy and a path to self-delusion. To this we answer that whether our meditation work has had any direct influence or not, these letters have formed a pretty reliable pointer to the shape of things to come. Even if we have had no hand in bringing them about, at least our readers have been accurately forewarned.

For our part we reply that we care for none of these things. We have received from tradition and intuition and psychic communications teachings which declare that if we will do certain things (i.e. group meditation along given lines), certain results will follow in the form of a new spirit in the heart of the race. Let those who are interested compare back numbers of these letters with current numbers of *The Times*.

We do not say these things in a spirit of boasting, but because a realisation of the potency of thought power is the first condition of its effectual use. If you believe that what you are doing is really powerful, the thought forms you construct will come up clear-cut on the astral plane, and will be highly dynamic. If you have no real faith in what you are doing, your thought-forms will have no clear outline. Therefore let us take the risk of being self-deluded because it may be that we really have done what we set out to do, and in consequence may succeed in carrying out our further plans.

> *14 June 1942 – Of a 17 ship convoy carrying supplies to Allied held Malta, only 2 get through German U-boat and dive bomber attacks.*

In the one hundred and twentieth letter Dion Fortune spells out in no uncertain terms the dynamics of attempts to use occult forces upon a group soul in a negative way. And it is of particular interest that one means of preserving health in the national soul is the restimulation of the Arthurian traditions.

LETTER 120
for June 14th 1942

In our last Letter we emphasised the power we possess to actualise our ideals by means of thought power if we set about it in the right way. We also considered the safeguards which prevent well-intentioned but wrongly conceived ideals from being brought to pass. Let us now consider the possibilities that a knowledge of these methods offers to those who are not merely well-intentioned though wrong-headed, but deliberately wish to poison the group mind of the race and make it helpless to defend itself, to divide it against itself, or to cause it to turn out of the main stream of progress into a backwater and run itself aground, leaving the way open for the advancement of its enemies.

We have seen how Fifth Column work destroyed the will to resist in France by sowing internal dissension and paralysing initiative. The Anglo-Saxon temperament is certainly not as suitable material as the Latin temperament for such activities, but we cannot count on complete immunity, and if the self-poisoning seeds really struck root, they would be proportionately harder to eradicate from the tougher material. We have given warning before on this point. We give warning again.

Although the group soul, like the blood stream, tends to destroy all alien influences that impinge upon it, there is a degree of massive infection which overcomes resistance. Moreover, if the attackers have the sense to concentrate on existing weaknesses and defects in national character and intensify them, instead of trying to turn us into a new and unnatural channel, a very great deal of disruption can be brought about.

Our principle protection against this form of attack lies in the fact that our enemies are aliens and do not understand our psychology; judging others by themselves, as everyone tends to do, their attempt to undermine our morale by broadcast propaganda is looked upon as light entertainment, and the BBC has not found it worth while to try to jam it, its ineptitude being its best antidote. But if disgruntled members of our own group soul took up the task, it would be a different story. They would operate from inside our psychic defences; they would strike along the true lines of cleavage in our group soul. What could be our defence against them?

Before answering this question, let us first ask another. Is there any reason to believe such activities are going on amongst us, or are we merely considering a possible contingency? We answer that there is good psychic reason to believe that such nuclei, or 'cells', as they are called, exist, but are at present on a small scale. The authorities, who are by no means oblivious to this kind of menace, made short work of the overt organisations in the early days of the war, and so paralysed their "Compromise and Co-operation" activities. But now, the war being already won on the Inner Planes, a new move is afoot to cause us to lose the peace. Where and how it is being developed we do not know: our readers may be assured that the information would be in the hands of the authorities if we did – but that something of an organised and directed nature is afoot we are certain. It is of a mental nature, and it can be countered mentally.

We are often asked how to counter mental attacks. We answer that the method is simple, as simple as the method of ridding a room of darkness by turning on the light. The erecting of psychic barriers is of no use against the enemy within the gates, who is turning against us our own weaknesses and exploiting legitimate grievances. How then can we prevent our morale from being undermined, our will from being deflected from its purpose, our inertia encouraged, our selfishness stimulated?

No negative methods can avail against the stimulation of septic foci within the body politic; nor can we cut them out in many cases without eradicating vital structures. Just as in the body the best defence is its own regenerative power, so in the group soul the best defence against this subtle poisoning is the stimulation of its most dynamic ideals.

To do this we must proceed according to the laws that govern the workings of the group mind, for it is the group mind that is being attacked. We must formulate clear-cut and brightly coloured mental pictures to embody our ideals, such pictures as are to be found in books for children, for the group mind is essentially a child mind, being the aggregate of the average, and humanity en masse is very undeveloped. These pictures must be dynamic, representing vigorous action, and they must relate to crowd action, not inner personal experience. They must represent an army with banners mobilised in the service of God. For such a purpose the conventional religious images are unsuitable; they are too personal and passive, but in the Arthurian Legends we have what we need. We have psychological material admirably adapted to our end, and a noble spiritual motif. Let us call up Arthur and his knights to lead the idealism of the nation, with the wise Merlin in the background to deal subtly with subtlety.

5 July 1942 – In the Crimea, Sevastopol finally falls to the Germans after 25 days of vicious hand-to-hand fighting.

Dion Fortune used her one hundred and twenty-third letter to look back once again upon the past work of the meditation group, one feels with a sense of achievement in a job that was approaching its conclusion.

LETTER 123
for July 5th 1942

When the war opened, the national morale had for the past year been at a lower ebb than it has ever been during my lifetime, which is not a short one. Never, even during the days when Zeppelins had us completely at their mercy, do I remember anything remotely resembling the panic caused by the war scare of September 1938. When war really came, however, a deeper stratum of the national consciousness began to assert itself, and morale steadied.

With the memory of those years behind me, I knew pretty well what to expect, and planned our progress of work accordingly; stopping our Magazine to conserve paper supplies for the Inner Group work; cutting down lectures and classes in expectation of transport restriction and call-up of personnel, and generally taking in sail. When the pressure came on it found us with a well barricaded basement into which we retired, and a programme which we have been able to carry out. Obeying instructions from the Inner Planes, we disappeared underground before the storm; in obedience to similar intimations we may be said, metaphorically speaking, to be cautiously coming up the area steps at the present moment. Let us hope it is a good omen, and that we are like the birds that are the farmer's weather guide.

Our first war term saw us with all activities stopped except a meditation circle organised for work on national morale. Week by week these Letters went out, giving instructions for the lines that work was to take. Those who have files of past Letters will observe how the phases through which our work passed kept some six months ahead of the phases through which the national consciousness passed. Equinox by equinox, that which had formulated on the Inner Planes during the preceding epoch came into manifestation on the physical plane. We worked on mass morale; we worked on the need for leaders, and on psychic attacks on our national morale. As time went on, and it became clear that the tide had turned on the Inner Planes, we concentrated our attention on the problems of reconstruction, indicating the lines it would move along and the pitfalls to be avoided. Gradually, week by week, the ground has been covered, till these papers form a pretty comprehensive blueprint of the world after the war, in so far as the internal affairs of this country are concerned. We were told from the commencement that the realisations thus obtained would impregnate the subconscious mind of the race, and be given forth from the rostrum of national life. We went forward in faith; but even so, it was with something of a shock that we realised that the task had been taken out of our humble hands by *The Times*, whose leading articles and correspondence columns – the recognised mirror of the national mind – gave our teachings an expression that was not only adequate but often verbatim, so that we find ourselves divided between a sense of the nearness and reality of great cosmic forces and an appreciation of the humour of the situation; and the mouse, having given birth to a mountain, cannot resist the temptation to admire the view. Except that it does not give meditation subjects, the Thunderer is carrying on the Esoteric Tradition worthily, and we see no occasion to compete with it.

We now propose to turn our attention to international reorganisation, and it will be interesting to observe whether the same sequence of events will ensue. Shall we once again formulate the abstract principles and see them in six months' time given concrete expression by those who have the ear of the nation? This has already happened in several instances, including the one on which we received the most adverse criticism of all – the abolition of the colour bar, which has been definitely laid down as one of the bases of the reorganisation of our colonial empire by the Colonial secretary. We must see it as individuals and as a group that this notable advance in Christian principle and biological practice does not get sidetracked by the dead weight of prejudice, and the more dynamic activities of the tendency to over-compensate our personal inferiorities by taking advantage of anyone whom circumstances have placed at a disadvantage. We suggest that people who hold strong views on this point should consider how they would feel if the Germans won the war and established themselves over here as the Herrenvolk, and they were to experience the working of racial discrimination from the wrong side of the barrier.

Let us remember, in these times of radical readjustment, that it is our duty to follow Truth wherever she may lead, and to place no barriers in her path, cost what it may.

THE MONTHLY LETTERS

In the October of 1942, just three years after the commencement of the weekly letters, the series came to an end. Friends and members of the Fraternity now received a Monthly Letter, which announced itself in the following terms, with a glance to the past and to the future.

MONTHLY LETTERS: EDITORIAL

To: The Friends and Members of the Fraternity of the Inner Light.

We are wondering whether you will be glad or sorry that the Weekly Letter is now to be issued monthly, and in expanded form, though still only the pale ghost of the original *Inner Light*. Our motives are partly to economise labour, and partly for a reason which we hope you will approve – in order that a more varied diet may be offered to our readers.

The weekly news sheet served a purpose during the critical early days of the war when morale wavered in the balance. It also had a steadying influence during the days of the Blitz. Moreover in those days – may they be gone for ever – it was a great advantage only to have to survive for one week, instead of four, between successive issues. Our readers stood a much better chance of getting the next number!

The present Monthly Letter contains the same amount of material as the Weekly Letters issued for the same period. It will contain a short editorial giving news of the activities of the Fraternity and any other matters of interest arising therefrom; an article on the lines of the familiar Weekly Letters, and two other articles, one dealing with the practical applications of occultism, and the other with its deeper issues. We thus hope to provide more varied fare of more lasting value and, as labour and paper supplies permit, to increase our boundaries till once more we reach magazine proportions and the *Inner Light* reincarnates.

October 1942 – 195,000 Allied troops begin the El Alamein offensive.

The first of the longer articles now featured was a general outline of occult teachings presented by the Fraternity of the Inner Light.

MONTHLY LETTER 1
for October 1942

THE OCCULT TEACHINGS

There are many different reasons why people study the occult teachings. Some like them because they are spectacular. Some love a mystery for its own sake. Some seek to penetrate the secrets of life and the Unseen. The best reason, and the most widespread, is a desire to understand life and the universe better in order that one may cope with it better, and it is to the people who read these lines for that reason that I would wish to speak. The sensationalist, the mystery-monger, and the intellectually inquisitive have no interest for me, and I have nothing that would interest them to offer. To the seeker after knowledge for the solution of life's problems, I would say: Come, let us reason together. Concerning the occult tradition, its teachings and their practical application, I can offer them the experience of a life spent on the Path. Nor will I ever mislead them by asserting anything to be a fact that I do not know to be such on good evidence, and I will always produce my evidence.

Between tradition, history and experience careful distinction must be made. Also between objective and subjective experience – objective experience gained through the five senses and subjective experience gained through the higher states of consciousness. Nevertheless, if we limited ourselves to the consideration of documented history and verifiable objective experience, we should miss much; for there is a wealth of information to be derived from tradition if we know how to interpret it and from subjective experience if we know how to countercheck it. The mistake is made when the different classes of data are confused and it is not clear from which source a particular statement is derived. This is unfair to the student, for it confuses his judgement. Moreover, the different classes of data have different evidential value, the objective and historical ranking first, and the traditional and subjective following after; to lead a student to believe something is historical which is traditional, or that something is objective which is subjective, is to take an unfair advantage of him, and indicates, if I may be pardoned for saying so, either ignorance or dishonesty on the part of the teacher who is guilty of it. Nevertheless, much data which ranks as traditional could be transferred to the ranks of the historical if the necessary scholarship were forthcoming; and much which is subjective could be given the same authority as objective assertions if an adequate psychological technique were applied. To do these things has long been one of our aims in the school of the Inner Light.

In the mass of literature and symbolism which we call the Occult Tradition we can discern a general pattern or plan. It falls into two broad divisions – teachings concerning the little understood powers of the human mind, and teachings concerning the mind side of Nature obtained by means of these little understood powers. The reader, when he first embarks upon such studies, will want to collect a certain amount of data for consideration. It is not possible for him to follow a train of philosophical thought concerning something of which he has no experience and has heard but the vaguest rumours. I will therefore try to supply some data drawn from my own experience.

An interest in occultism usually starts in the realm of subjective experience. People feel vaguely that there must be some kind of hidden reality stretching out beyond what the senses reveal to them. Moreover the tradition of a mysterious wisdom leading on to power is so widespread that there can be few who have never heard of it, even it be only in the form of sensational fiction. Sometimes there comes a sense of the actual presence of an invisible reality; sometimes there comes an intellectual realisation of its possible presence – whichever it is – that is the starting point of the Quest.

The awareness of the existence of an invisible reality, and the gathering of knowledge and experience concerning it begins as gradually as the dawn of consciousness in a newborn child. Indeed, an initiate is often referred to as twice-born in contradistinction to the once-born, who are aware of their physical existence only, the second birth being into the realms of the higher consciousness, where the seeker has to begin at the beginning, even as the new-born babe, and amass data through experience and interpret it in the light of a growing understanding.

If people would be content to begin at the beginning with the small things of personal psychic experience, they would progress much faster than they do if they wait for something drastic in the way of manifestation to happen to them. We all have had experience of intuitions, of minor instances of telepathy, or of an awareness of the subtle atmosphere of persons, places or things brought about by mind power. Let us make a start from our own personal experiences and build on those, for it is out of these that the higher ranges of the occult powers are developed; all the elaborate technique of operative occultism is but designed to develop and utilise and co-ordinate those small seeds of unseen powers. "First the seed, then the ear, then the full corn in the ear." However well the field be tilled, if there is no seed therein, it is barren ground.

Then, you will ask, who sows the seed? Is there spontaneous generation on the psychic plane? No, there is nothing of the sort, any more than there is spontaneous generation of something out of nothing on the physical plane. The psychic faculties are normal in a primitive stage of development of humanity; they become overlaid by the physical senses and the rational mind as evolution progresses, and they become correlated therewith after a certain amount of progress has been made. It is the correlation of those lost subtle senses of primitive man with the rational consciousness of civilised man which constitutes true psychic development as distinguished from the retrogressive psychism which arises in certain pathological mental conditions due to dissociation of the personality.

Such a concept, however, turns upon a belief in reincarnation. This is the real keystone of occult studies. If reincarnation is not a fact, then is all our hope of initiation in vain, for no one can make such progress in a single life as would enable him to pass through all the stages of evolution and achieve its goal. Life after life, the initiate believes, he comes back to earth, not only with another body but with another personality, his spiritual self alone being the unifying factor; life by life he recapitulates his previous development of consciousness, just as he has already recapitulated the life of the race in his prenatal existence; passing from the unicellular to the multicellular, from fish to frog to mammal, finally to be born in the human form. But if he has once acquired extended consciousness, he will retain an awareness of its possibility even if the powers themselves have to be awakened by laborious training and exercise. Those who have an inner certainty of the existence of invisible realities, and an inner urge to pursue this study and seek its experience, have certainly been on the Path in other lives, and it is subconscious memories that they are drawing upon and are driven by. In such persons there is a nostalgia for the Unseen which will not let them rest; a divine discontent with materialism, whether as a philosophy or as a science. The seed is in their souls when they are born, and only awaits its due season to germinate.

Those who undertake the preparation of students for initiation soon learn to distinguish between the once-born and the twice-born – the barren field and the sown, and on the gradings thus made we base the training we give to our students. There is an irreducible minimum which all must have in order that they may acquire a working knowledge of the system we use, for Mystery systems vary as between the different

Traditions, and even the different schools of a Tradition, and training in one does not admit a student ready made to the higher grades of another. Once the irreducible minimum has been acquired, however, progress is by attainment and not by seniority.

The first Monthly Letter also revealed a hitherto well kept secret: the mediumship of Dion Fortune. By way of example there followed a long communication received by such means. This is the voice of one of the Masters, or Elder Brethren, or Inner Plane Adepti, to which in the past Dion Fortune had often referred. The difference in tone between this mediumistically received communication and Dion Fortune's own style of writing is noticeable. In content and intent this example appears to be a general address intended for those who aspire to initiatory training within the Fraternity. The pattern of individual growth is illustrated by reference to Masonic symbolism, of the rough stone from the quarry being shaped and polished before being hoisted to its rightful place in the temple structure.

THE MEDIUMSHIP OF DION FORTUNE

The mediumship of Dion Fortune has been a well-kept secret within the Inner Group of the Fraternity, but it has recently been decided to make a secret of it no longer in order that certain of the teachings thus received may be made available for all who follow the Path.

The following address was received through her mediumship, and is here given verbatim. It is hoped that similar addresses, and extracts from others, will be available for each issue of the Monthly letter. There is a great wealth of unpublished material thus received which will be released for publication.

Greetings, my children:
Tonight I want to talk to you about an aspect of the Mystery Work which is very practical, and upon which the whole super-structure rests, and that is the character and condition of the individual Members of the Fraternity; for they are the blocks of stone of which the Temple is builded, and as such are represented upon the Altar.

The newly admitted neophyte is the Rough Ashlar, squared but not yet trimmed or polished. The initiate who has completed the Three Degrees of the Lesser Mysteries is represented by the Perfect Ashlar, polished and lewissed. This teaches you that in order to gain admission to even the First Degree of these Mysteries you must stand four-square, firmly, upon a level basis. This basis of character is to be wrought upon by the diligent work of the mind. The will plays a part, but not the only part, or even the most considerable part.

There is a skilled technique in the Mysteries by means of which Rough Ashlar of character is polished into the Perfect Ashlar. In the stone this polishing is achieved firstly by the use of the chisel and mallet, knocking off the rough masses. This may be likened to life experience. Then follows the work of polishing – the steady friction which may be likened to the work of meditation.

In the Outer Court you are taught first how to acquire knowledge by meditation. In the Inner Court you begin to learn how to acquire power by meditation, and the first power you acquire is power over yourself, without which no other powers can be handled. This is your fulcrum. You are not taught how to acquire power over yourself until you have gained the knowledge which teaches you how to use that power over yourself rightly – not doing violence to your known nature nor yet setting up a deformity or unbalance within it. You must understand life in all its aspects before you are competent to apply power to your own nature.

First, then, realise that your being is divided into two parts – the Higher Self and the Lower Self; the Higher Self building around the nucleus of the Divine Spark evolving throughout evolution – the Lower Self building around the nucleus of the basic angle in the Triangle of the Higher Self – the unit of incarnation.

When, upon the Path, you are striving after that state which shall enable you to give expression to your Higher Self in the Personality, by means of a certain technique you can aid the process.

Firstly, realise this, that while in incarnation your consciousness is focused in the Personality by means of sensation and emotion. Consequently, if you desire to alter the focus of consciousness, you must acquire control of sensation and emotion, and learn at will to reduce them to a minimum. There is an irreducible minimum beyond which you cannot reduce them.

In order to achieve such control you work firstly upon the emotions. To achieve control of these you imagine yourself to be your Individuality. You raise consciousness to that level by meditating upon the evolution of the Divine Spark which is the nucleus of your being. You realise it as issuing from the dark night of the unmanifest into manifestation, where it is a light in darkness. You conceive of your experiences as that

Spark through the earlier phases of evolution, circling with the Rings and Rays in limitless space. You imagine the formulation of Form and the great Tides moving in the Cosmos. You picture to yourself the dim soul asleep in unconsciousness, overshadowing its shadowy vehicle. You picture the slow contacting of consciousness through the sensory organs of that vehicle – its crude sensations – its primeval desires – food, fighting and mating. And so you conceive of the rise of consciousness from the primordial slime, up through the bestiality of the primaeval human into the slow dawn of culture: the rise of the ancient civilisations – the great Pagan cults close to nature, that train your soul with human sacrifice and orgy: the steady progression of humanity from culture to culture: the refining away of the brute; the manifesting of the human; the overshadowing of the angelic.

So does man rise; coming from God, and returning to God as a god. And remember, it is the garnered essence of all these experiences that makes man as he is today, and you have missed none of them, and they are all latent in your deeper memories.

On this basis you build; into these primordial and primeval depths as into a rich and fertile soil you strike your roots downwards, that you may raise the Flower of Life above them. No root – no flower: and your flower is in proportion to your root, as any gardener will tell you. Reach deeply and consciously down into the primordial, and draw thence the Flower of Life. Do not fear the primordial, though it is terrible: do not despise it or condemn it, though it is base. In Elemental strength must you be rooted.

From blood sacrifice and orgy the Mysteries arose. Today we work them on a higher arc, but the principles do not change. Upon the principles of sacrifice and polarity the Mysteries are worked, changing from the physical, to the astral, to the mental, and to the spiritual as the ages pass.

By thus transferring the focus of consciousness by the work of the imagination, backward up the Great River of Time to its source – down the Great River of Time in its flowing, so do you learn to identify yourself with your Higher Self, realising the richness of the background from which you arose.

Then consider the personality of incarnation, viewed from this standpoint. See it in perspective: realise that evolution stretches before you just as it stretches behind you, and that the life of the Personality is but a day between a sleep and a sleep. See it in perspective and in proportion. You have had many personalities – you shall have many more; personalities are ephemeral.

There is but one thing that matters concerning the personality – that you should work out in that brief span between birth and death your measure of evolutionary experience. And how shall you do this? By realising what manner of personality has been given you to work with in this life, and what you need to do with it during the opportunity thus afforded you for development and progress. Consider, then, your own personality in the light of your evolutionary past, and remember that in the space between conception and maturity you recapitulate that past – biologically as the unborn – psychologically as the immature. Through all the phases of your past you go until the full stature of your development is achieved as a fully grown and mature-minded human being. In each life you should add something to your stature; and it is your task to discover what this may be, and how you shall fulfil your destiny; for each one comes into incarnation with a destiny to fulfil, and this destiny you read in your own heart by learning what it is towards which it impels you in your deepest self, when you are true to the life urge within you – not what custom directs, but what life requires of you.

Dare to be your true self in your own mind, even if the circumstances of your life deny you the outward expression thereof, for action in the outer world is but a mirror in which we see reflected back to us that which is within. Be true to yourself within yourself, and life will reflect opportunity back to you. Deny your true self within yourself, and life will reflect back to you frustration. Only when you are your true self, only when you have come to terms with your real nature, can you stand upright upon your feet, in equilibrium, security and inner peace.

Thus do you perform the process of self-examination in the light of cosmic time; and then, having examined and adjusted yourself to your true self, you take your personality in hand and make it your mask. Like the magical images in the Temples of Atlantis, you make of your personality your instrument of expression. You mould and fashion it: you work upon it until it becomes the Perfect Ashlar – the perfected instrument. But it cannot be your instrument so long as consciousness is centred in your feelings and desires. Learn to disregard these feelings. Live in your inner self. Learn to break in your desires, that they may carry you forward on the Path like a strong beast of burden. And as to the sensations of the body, master the art of relaxation, whereby they are reduced to a minimum, freeing the consciousness for the higher contemplation.

The work of polishing the rough block of temperament into the finished Ashlar of character is achieved by dwelling in meditation upon the ideal you have set yourself, and by thought control. Control the imagination and you control the emotions. Build daily; build steadily; build systematically. Do not accept your feelings as your masters: learn that the feelings can be mastered by the higher mind, and bring them into subjection to your directing judgement. This is the work of the Exempt Adept, who has freed himself from the bondage of his feelings. For the work of the higher magic you must have such thought control, so that you can regulate the imagination, and through imagination the feelings.

When you have worked the Rough Ashlar into the Perfect Ashlar, it is then ready to be lewissed. The lewis or cramp is the ring-bolt of metal which is set in it, by means of which it can be hoisted into position in the edifice. The lewis or ring-bolt represents the psychic faculties which link the personality with the higher consciousness and enable it to perceive with the eyes of the Higher Self on the Inner Planes.

Thus must you work on yourselves to be stones in the edifice of the Temple. The Exempt Adept is characterised by his poise and unruffled serenity and peace; for peace that cannot be disturbed is the sign of self mastery. The Magus is master of himself before he can be Master of the Lodge: otherwise he will wreak destruction with his magical power.

It is through this inner serenity and peace that the ease in working comes which was indicated to you as the ideal at which you should aim, having achieved efficiency. It is something to achieve the control of the outer expression of the feelings – this is demanded of civilised man in social life – but inner control of the feelings which harmonises them into peace is demanded of the initiate for his magical work.

Work upon yourselves till you learn the lesson of peace. Accept the tasks and the conditions which your destiny allots in each incarnation. Work contentedly and faithfully within your limits – for not in one life can you expect to compass the whole range of evolutionary experience. Adapt your way of life to the means available on the physical plane, but in your Inner Life have freedom – the freedom of the whole arc of the heavens and the whole range of evolutionary time: freedom of realisation, and freedom in the building power of the imagination.

Thus shall the soul to be freed from its shackles – disciplined in matter, but free-winged in the ether. In self-realisation find your inner freedom. How much or how little of your realisation can be given expression in a single incarnation is immaterial. You have many incarnations – all you need – in which to work out your realisations. Never let your incarnation limit your realisation, for it is your realisation that builds your incarnations through the power of the imagination. What you realise in this incarnation will be expressed in the next incarnation. Your present life teaches you the discipline of form. Learn to work within the limits set you by circumstances; but the creative imagination is free, within the limits of realisation, to build for the future.

November 1942 – Faced by the seemingly unstoppable advance of Montgomery's tanks and troops, Rommel's Afrika Korps is forced to retreat. The Allied Expeditionary Force lands in North Africa.

It may here be of interest to refer back to Dion Fortune's comment at the end of 1941, in Letter No. 95, to the effect that she was withdrawing from Outer Court activity to some extent, in order to undertake more inner work. This type of mediumistic work was plainly a part of it, but not always in terms of a general address as in the last example. Communication could be more personal and specific, as may be seen from the following notes that were made by a close associate at what was plainly an interview with an Inner Plane communicator via Dion Fortune's mediumship.

It commences with a personal note to C.R. Cammell, the editor of *Light*, the significance of which is no longer apparent, but which serves to show that all such communication from Inner Plane sources was not confined to general teaching or cosmic abstractions, but that personal advice and guidance was available when appropriate.

We then have a series of remarks upon the international situation at the time – which happens to be the eve of the fall of Singapore. Whether this is an example of prophecy is open to question; by the time this communication was given the fact may already have happened, or certainly been imminent.

This is in the context of comments on a number of more distant events that are envisaged, although these are in the tone of speculative thought rather than specific predictions. Some of what was then envisaged has come to pass, the loss of British imperial and colonial possessions for example, which would have been by no means obvious at the time. Other ideas, such as international control of means of communication and transport have not, although there is still plenty of time for this to happen as the world shrinks with the advance of technology, and international cooperation becomes more imperative in various areas of concern. This type of Inner Plane communication also gives us an insight into the general drift of Dion Fortune's latter Weekly Letters, which become more concerned with the challenge of post-war reconstruction than with the press of current events.

The communication concludes with a more symbolically developed sequence of remarks upon aerial warfare in an age of Air. It seems likely from these comments that they come from one of Dion Fortune's Inner Plane communicators who had been killed at Ypres in the First World War, and who would have had his views on the training of Generals. It was a firm belief proclaimed by one senior commander of the time that air power would never replace cavalry. This strategic theory has hardly stood the test of time but it is doubtful whether argument along the lines of the communicator's symbolically based comment would ever cut much ice in conservative military circles, then or now.

One might also note that the communicator, by implication, does not seem to anticipate that the warfare currently in hand is likely to be the last on Earth. In this his powers of prediction have certainly not been found wanting.

Communication received February 14th, 1942.

Tell C.R.C. that organised opposition is at an end. He should strive to reconcile himself with those who opposed him, but there is one woman, the centre of the opposition, who will probably prove irreconcilable.

On the International Situation:
There is no need to be anxious; a failure in the morale of the Allies is the only thing that could lose the war and that is unlikely.

The tides of destruction or rather purgation are not intrinsically evil. Evil has no Cosmic support; but these tides test and prove all things; they expose and wash away all that is weak and effete.

This is a period of reform.

You will observe they are seeking out all the weak spots in the Allied organism. They are re-exposing the effete leadership of the nation and they are tearing up by the roots the Colonial Empire in Asia. There you have peoples capable of a higher culture who have not been afforded the opportunity for that culture, but have been exploited in the interests of commerce. That which we lose now will not be restored to us.

(Asked if the inference was that it would be wrong to fight a long war to recover possession the answer was: Yes.)

Singapore is going. *(N.B. The news of the fall of Singapore was announced on Sunday, Feb. 15th, 1942.)*

The rightful owners will resume ownership but there will be strategic points all over the world which will be held by the United Nations for international commerce and international policing and they will be mandated. For the whole of the New Age turns on the concept of the ownership of the land by the people versus the ownership of the people by the land. So you will see a great many places hitherto under English ownership reverting to the original owners. But they will not be under Axis ownership. Because the soil owns the people, not the people the soil; therefore there are very big changes coming in the organisation of this country.

I think that in the near future Germany will collapse in Europe and that England will lose her foothold in the Far East, never to recover it. There will be drastic changes in the Government and in social organisation and it will be all to the good.

The subsequent reconstruction will be based on an agreement between those like-minded powers inviting the adherence of all who share their views. There will be arrangements between them on the interchange of commodities and the organisation of law and order and it will be implemented by means of a network of international trade routes over which goods and persons will move freely in the name of the Associated Nations and without regard to local frontiers.

(It was here pointed out that there was considerable difference of opinion as to whether Germany could be associated with the free nations after the war and the communicator said: "Prussia is not like-minded but there may be parts of Germany which are.")

There will be a ruling hegemony of the nations who win the war and these trade routes will be international; and at strategic points will be established great depots of exchange – international markets. These will also be centres of an international police-force maintaining order.

This trade will move freely over the whole globe so that access to the sea will not matter and nations will not need to fight for it.

The sea will be the international highway of all nations and depots, harbours and strategic points will be held by the authority of the Commonwealth of Nations just as England holds Gibraltar.

Equally, international highways, railways and inland waterways will be under international control.

Thus in losing her strong points in the Far East, England sacrifices nothing save causes of friction and sources of expense.

The Commonwealth of Free Nations will secure strategic points all over the world to prevent future aggression and to aid the development of trade.

And the test of righteousness is Universality.

It is the welfare of the common man all over the earth that is the basis on which the strength of the Commonwealth of Nations rests and whom it exists to serve.

The Aquarian Age develops in the element of Air. It is in the air that the keys are to be sought. The wars of the present and of the future will be fought in the air, with land and sea forces as supporting units; not the Air Force as the support of the land and sea forces. That is the key to all the disasters suffered. England cannot win on land; she is a sea and air power.

It is in the air that the future lies because Aquarius is an airy Sign. It is not a case of air power supporting an advancing army but of air power making the attack and the land forces consolidating the gains; therefore the strategy of victory in this war must be based on the conditions of aerial combat. The land forces must be considered as supporting forces; the land forces cannot operate without the air force but air forces can operate without land forces but cannot consolidate their gain.

The Air Marshals must learn to use the land forces to follow up and consolidate the gains obtained in the air, which is the battle field of the future. To instruct the Generals in the use of the air arm in conjunction with the work of the troops would be a waste of time, even if it were possible to instruct a General. When a man holding General's rank was trained he was not a General and you can't teach an old dog new tricks. The trouble is that the men in command of the fighting forces are Pisceans by virtue of their seniority; wherever their conditions of the earlier age prevail they are competent; wherever the conditions of the New Age prevail they are unable to perceive their nature and are therefore unable to grapple with them. The war will be fought and won in the realms of the air and of the mind – that meaning in the sphere of morale.

The democracies belong to the New Age; the Axis Powers represent the recrudescence of ebbing forces whose day is past; therefore their time in any case is short. For the tides of life are against them.

The flash-back of the previous extract provides a glimpse into the informal inner/outer plane relationship that pertained to the inner recesses of the Fraternity. From this we can appropriately turn to an article in the second Monthly Letter which provides detailed remarks (from an Inner Plane source) on how such communication is made, and some of the consequences that may arise from it.

MONTHLY LETTER 2
for November 1942

MODUS OPERANDI OF TRANCE COMMUNICATIONS

Received through the mediumship of Dion Fortune.

It is quite simple if you understand the rationale of hypnosis. The medium, by first relaxing completely and then concentrating on the image of the communicator, disconnects the conscious mind from the subconscious. This is done by gathering the focus of attention to a single point and holding it there until the mind ceases to register. This disconnects the levels of consciousness. The point on which attention is concentrated is the image of the communicator.

Consequently, when the directing mind is disconnected, as it were, the subconsciousness has this image imprinted on it.

The communicating entity, who is a mind without a body, visualises his own image, and the two images being identical, a telepathic rapport with the medium's subconsciousness is established.

The subconscious mind of the medium then dramatises the personality of the control. The control conveys ideas to the subconscious mind of the medium telepathically. These ideas are archetypal or abstract. That is why it is so difficult to convey names or numbers. It is the dramatised, artificial personality created by the mind of the medium which talks to you. If there is within the scope of the medium's knowledge the material out of which the trance address can be made, it is utilised. If the material is lacking,a symbolic method of presentation has to be used.

Persons who are naturally of mediumistic type are quite different from the trained medium used by a Mystery School. The trained medium is taught how to dissociate the levels of a well-knit mind, and how to take the initial steps in the dramatisation of the personality of the communicator. These acts are voluntary, whereas in the natural medium they are involuntary; and that person is only saved from the consequences of dissociation of personality and the dramatisation of the secondary personality by the intervention of a spirit guide. In the absence of a spirit guide the dissociation of the personality and development of the secondary personalities follow the ordinary course of a psychopathic manifestation. It frequently happens that a medium of this type, who has worked well under a spirit guide, may lose contact with that guide and then become merely a schizophrenic. Or the guide may sometimes be in touch with the medium, sometimes not, and so the quality of the trance will vary.

Trance communications should always be judged by their intrinsic content, because once the image has been built, the subconscious mind of the medium can produce a perfectly good simulacrum of the communicator.

In the light of this explanation you will see why it is that a medium of an unevolved type of personality has for control a child or a savage, for the limitations of the medium's personality are such that these are the adequate presentations. Such persons, being themselves children at heart, the communicator is limited by the calibre of the medium, save in the matter of symbolic presentation, of which the prophets of the Old Testament afford an example.

The question of language presents no real difficulty because the ideas are formulated by the control in terms of the higher mind which has an abstract type of mentation. The translation into concrete terms takes place in the medium's subconscious. Terms or names with which the medium is unfamiliar have either to be spelt out by the communicator or communicated phonetically.

The personality of the communicator, however, if well dramatised, should come through very clearly and be able to establish direct telepathic contact with the minds of the sitters. This plays a very important part in their development.

Are they to know how questions (written) are answered? If the answer causes their hearts to burn, the link is made. That is the test. Personal advice is seldom given. You are to judge. It is a question of the principles underlying a case (with which we deal). For those who are high in the Mysteries things can be done to facilitate their work that could not be considered in the lower grades. Intervention from the higher planes concerns the nature of Destiny and whether they can co-operate intelligently. The laws of destiny are mastered by observance.

In regard to a written question, if you bring it to me from someone who is seeking instruction and I answer it, a link is established, and in due course that person may be accepted for personal instruction. The results are twofold. The teaching of the doctrine is one thing, and can be conveyed by the written word, but the power of the Presence is another thing, and the written word only partially conveys it.

X is a man with mystical contacts, and illuminated. He is the holder of a position; he invoked, and 'I am come in answer to his prayer'. It is not only a matter of what practical services he can give, but a matter of his past (incarnations) and his contacts. Therefore do not consider it from a purely utilitarian point of view. You know the old story of the person who uses the magical words and is startled by the appearance of the spirit?

This man, using a true formula, made contact; much or little may come of it, but he is entitled to his opportunity. Results are his affair. It is not your responsibility, nor mine. You and I are channels, not sources of contact; deal with him as originally planned; make no difficulty; let the matter work itself out. Give him the opportunity as promised; what use he makes of it, or fails to make of it, is his affair. The man who gives the correct password and knocks at the Door of the Mysteries may not be refused, even if he gives them in ignorance. But in this case they were not given in ignorance, but in a moment of vision. Let that impulse then set going take its course. A man has more than one incarnation. 'Give to him that asketh of you'. I am thinking of the help he needs, which should be given to him without question. Consider him as a soul lost in a dark forest who will go down into grievous darkness if he cannot have a helping hand. You may have wondered at the form my help took; that, being arrogant, he met with arrogance. 'With the froward I will show myself froward'.

What is said is not forgotten, and it will do its work; for it is a law of my being that I may not deny truth, and truth takes the responsibility. I may often have occasion to say to people what they may not like; it is not for you to soften the blow or turn aside the surgeon's knife.

December 1942 – Following successful experiments with nuclear fission, Roosevelt orders a stop to the sharing of atomic secrets with the British.

Dion Fortune's use of mediumship in esoteric work brings into question its use in the Spiritualist movement, where it is used in a different context and largely for a different purpose. There had been an uneasy period in the attitude of the Fraternity towards Spiritualism, leading at one point to a ban on members taking part in any such activities. This had led to the resignation of those who felt compromised by such a ruling. A considerable amount of re-thinking had obviously gone on in the meantime, resulting in a long article on the subject by Dion Fortune in the third Monthly Letter. She had also, over the past few months, started to give lectures at the headquarters of the Marylebone Spiritualist Association.

MONTHLY LETTER 3
for December 1942

THE FRATERNITY OF THE INNER LIGHT AND SPIRITUALISM

It is desirable at the present juncture to make clear to our members and friends the position of the Fraternity of the Inner Light with regard to Spiritualism. To those who have knowledge of both movements it is obvious that they are the two sides of the same coin. Spiritualism is empirical Occultism. Occultism is traditional Spiritualism. The methods and tone of the two movements differ, the one being propagandist and the other exclusive. In the past both had their separate tasks to perform, and could only perform them separately. Occultism had to keep alive and increase our heritage of psychic knowledge, and Spiritualism had to introduce the same concepts to the popular mind in a form that could be appreciated by people whose past incarnations had given them no subconscious aptitude for understanding the invisible realities and who were making their first approach to the Path. Both movements were under the jurisdiction of the Great White Lodge, but were carried on by different groups of Masters on the Inner Planes and their servers and pupils on the physical plane.

Independent organisation was necessary, as the one movement aimed at the widest possible publicity in order to influence popular opinion (which it has done successfully), and the other still needed to remain in seclusion till public opinion had undergone the preparation that was the work of the Spiritualist movements. During the last great war Spiritualism came in to its own and accomplished its mission, and its contribution to human thought is now an accepted part of our culture. In this war Occultism is coming into its own in turn, consolidating the ground pioneered by Spiritualism.

The Masters of the Great White Lodge have given instructions to the Brethren charged with the direction of both movements that the time for co-operation has come, and the two movements are to make contact at their periphery, like two circles meeting and slowly blending. There will for a long while yet be much of the Spiritualistic movement which has no tinge of the occult philosophy but limits itself to research into psychic phenomena and the proof of survival, furnishing enquirers with evidence and the bereaved with consolation. There will also be a certain proportion of Occultism, the Greater Mysteries, which will continue to function in seclusion because the world is not yet ready for it. But there will be an unbroken line of approach from the propagandist aspect of the Spiritualistic movement right through to the arcana of Occultism. Both movements will be enriched thereby; the vast, undeveloped wealth of tradition being placed at the disposal of Spiritualists, and the highly specialised gifts of psychics and mediums being made available for the work of practical Occultism.

It is desired by the Masters that every effort should be made, both individually and collectively, to break down the distrust and antagonism that has so long prevailed between the two movements; it has no justification, unless "trade competition" be considered a justification. Occultists should familiarise themselves with the methods of the Spiritualist séance; they would find that they were by no means on unfamiliar ground, had much to learn from a more highly developed technique than is customary in their own movement. Spiritualists equally should be offered opportunities of gaining first-hand experience of practical Occultism.

Having thus explained the essential unity of the two movements, we also need to make clear the factors in which they differ, not through antagonism, but through specialisation. Spiritualism is concerned primarily with the task of bringing the subtler forms of existence into touch with the physical plane through the work of its mediums and psychics, whose development for this purpose has been the object of a vast amount of study and accumulated data of experience. Occultism, on the other hand, teaches those who pursue it to function on the Inner Planes themselves, and as these levels of manifestation are the planes of causation in respect of the physical plane, it is possible, within certain limits varying with the attainments of the individual, to influence conditions on the physical plane. No hard and fast line can be drawn between Spiritualist and Occult activities in these matters; for it is obvious to all who have any practical experience of both movements that they overlap, but broadly speaking, the two movements will be found to have differentiated along the lines described because they have specialised along those lines, not because their activities are mutually exclusive. That Occultism has owed much to mediumship is witnessed by the tradition of the Oracles and the well known life story of Madame Blavatsky; after whose death C.W. Leadbeater, her student, continued to keep open the lines of psychic communication. The lesser known history of MacGregor Mathers, the great English occultist, who used his wife as his medium, and his collaborator, Brodie Innes, who was himself mediumistic, confirm the tradition.

The question is frequently asked as to whether the Fraternity of the Inner Light makes use of mediums and psychics, and whether Dion Fortune, its Warden, is herself a medium. Hitherto information has been refused on this point to all save those in the higher grades of its own organisation. The time has now come, however, to give an answer. The Fraternity trains its students, to begin with, in the philosophy of the Esoteric Tradition and in the practice of meditation. Advancing beyond this grade, they are developed psychically and taught how to enter the Inner Planes by the traditional Paths. Advancing further, they study the art of operating the astral forces. All members take their part in the skrying (or clairvoyance) according to capacity, but are not encouraged to act as mediums for each other, as they are expected to go on to the Inner Planes themselves and make direct contact with the Masters, by means of the meditation methods by which they are trained. A line of direct communication is always kept open, however, but it is operated from the Inner Planes, and the members of the Fraternity do not sit for development in mediumship. Dion Fortune at present holds this office, which she took over from her predecessor and teacher, who likewise received it from his teacher, but individual members have from time to time, according to capacity, had experiences that have enabled them to test for themselves the Inner Plane contacts claimed for their Fraternity. These have also been counter-checked recently by mediums belonging to well known Spiritualist organisations.

The Fraternity has never used psychic phenomena as a proof of the validity of its teaching, knowing that these phenomena, like miracles, prove nothing save their own existence and that teachings must be judged by their intrinsic content. The lines of communication with the Inner Planes which are used by occultists are more sensitive than those used by Spiritualists, and more easily disturbed by adverse psychic influences; consequently their work has to be guarded by the traditional seclusion, and our friends must forgive us if there is a certain reticence about our reference to them. No doubt we shall in time profit by our contact with the Spiritualist movement to improve our technique and throw open more widely the doors of the Mysteries. At present we must feel our way and make haste slowly in practical matters involving a break with age-old tradition.

It may be as well to say a few words here concerning the use of ceremonial, which plays so important a part in Occultism but of which Spiritualism has hitherto only so far availed itself in a very minor degree. The arrangement of the sitters in a circle, the playing of soft music, the singing of hymns and the prayers of dedication and invocation commonly practised in home circles are ritual of a simple kind; but there are aspects of ritual little realised by those who have not seen them, and their beauty and power bring through manifestations which, if subjected to psychic investigation, should yield very interesting results.

At the present moment, with the war hampering all our activities and dispersing our trained personnel, it is difficult, in fact almost impossible, for us to work these rituals in a way that shall do them justice, and ceremonial badly done is a very undesirable thing; but when happier days come, and they are already showing signs of dawning, we look forward to developments from the sharing of the Occult and the Spiritualist resources, and co-operation with other Occult organisations which shall enrich the field of human knowledge for all men, and not just for one secret fraternity. This can only come about through generosity and open-mindedness on both sides. In some quarters we have met with these truly Christian qualities in an abundance that has led to most happy relationships; in others, they have been regrettably lacking. May we be allowed to say that if we are right in believing that it is the will of those Great Ones behind both movements that there should be brotherly co-operation between their respective servers, then those organisations that will not co-operate will find themselves left behind by the march of events, and that the wonderful influx of new life that is flowing down upon us all from the Inner Planes will be unable to penetrate channels that are closed to brotherhood.

We, for our part, are not set in our ideas; we want to learn as well as to teach. There are things I wrote of Spiritualism twenty years ago which, in the light of wider experience, I would not write today, and to cite these as evidence against me is to deny the possibility of human progress. I was trained in a rigid tradition, and it has taken many years to win to a position where I could stand on my own feet, beholden to none, and with none in a position to call me to account under the Oath of the Mysteries for my actions. That is now my happy position, and I offer and ask for the pooling of knowledge by all who have anything to pool. Only thus can knowledge advance, and there is no religion higher than the Truth. Loyalty to Truth ranks higher than loyalty to personalities. I am no believer in the right to give oneself a dispensation to break a solemn oath, but I am also no believer in the right to enforce that oath in a spirit of exclusiveness and pride of possession. The occult fraternities may be proud of their long descent and gorgeous rites, but true wisdom is humble, and compassionate to human needs, and if in our secret archives we have, as I know we have, knowledge that could lead on to human betterment and relieve human suffering, we have no right to guard it as our secret heritage, but should make it available for all who need it.

> *January 1943 – The Germans finally surrender to Soviet forces in Stalingrad. Adolf Hitler orders the total mobilisation of the German people. Authorities can now order men and women to undertake any task necessary for the defence of the Reich.*

Arthurian symbolism was prominent in the early Letters, and in Letter 87, with its associated meditation on 'the waking of Arthur', Dion Fortune had drawn attention to its importance in the protection and vitality of the group soul of the nation. This line of work was later followed up by another brilliant medium and psychic within the Society of the Inner Light, Margaret Lumley Brown. Some of the early Inner Plane communication on the subject, as received by Dion Fortune, is to be found in the fourth and fifth Monthly Letters.

MONTHLY LETTER 4 & 5
for January & February 1943

TEACHING CONCERNING ARTHURIAN LEGENDS

Received through the mediumship of Dion Fortune.

I.

There is a matter that has been dominating your minds. Whatever is dominating the minds of those who come makes a stepping-off place. Thus if you want consecutive teaching you should fill your minds with the previous communications.

However, there is no waste of time in considering the bearing of scholarship upon the study of the Mysteries in general and, in particular, the Arthurian legends of which the Grail forms a part. The same type of story can be traced through many a mythology and scholars collate them, tracing the common factors in widely diversified schools and traditions. This is valuable because knowledge is never entirely without value.

First there is the question of collating legends with one another and with other traditions. Take the Grail or the Wounded King. There are many versions of the wounded King within the Arthurian tradition and many versions of the Grail story spread through other traditions. There are certain factors in the human mind which are common to all men, and when expressed in symbolism, will be expressed in related symbolism. There are others which have been developed within a specific school of doctrine.

The Grail story concerns the common needs of all mankind; the healing of the Wounded King by a specific method concerns a particular school of doctrine. The one is a primary, the other a secondary legend. In dealing with the mythology of the Mysteries the scholarship required should afford a background that covers the whole range of cognate thought so that you can judge of a given story whether it is a primary legend with its roots in the deepest instinctual level of human need, the level from which dreams arise, or whether it is the creation of the conscious mind to point a moral.

There should be a scholarship adequate to the understanding of the sources of these two types of material. To understand a primary legend you need knowledge of the human mind at its primitive level both in the present and in the past. Knowledge of its primary level in the present is to be sought in analytical psychology; knowledge of its primitive level in the past is to be sought, first, in the records of primitive mankind in ancient days, and secondly in the customs and beliefs of peoples who retain their primitive level of culture. The sources of secondary legends are literary, to be sought in the superficial meaning of primary legends interpreted in the light of contemporary influences, religious and cultural.

So, therefore, in studying a given story, scholarship is needed to determine the date of its first appearance. Does it go back to the archaic forms of the traditions and the earliest records of them? Does it first appear in a primitive form, expressed in terms of primitive thought, and are there analogous stories in other traditions? Or does it appear only at a later date in a sophisticated form and is it peculiar to the Arthurian tradition?

This will enable you to determine and distinguish what is fundamental and valid, the work of true seers, from what is superficial and misleading, the work of the moralising theologian or literary fancy. I want to correct one point: the earlier form is the work of many minds – the racial mind, not the individual seer. There are however many seers at all levels of culture, and true seership may shine through a purely literary work.

Now let us trace the matter historically. The earliest form of all legends is in the work of the story teller to the tribe gathered around the camp fire; it is childish imagining concerning the nature of things. In the next stage the minds of the priestly caste work over the primitive stories. At a later stage a new concept of religion may arise and push aside the primitive. Or conquest by invaders may bring a new race and their culture into influence, and the old culture will be forgotten except by the story-tellers among the submerged people. So the primitive tradition returns into the custody of the bards again. Then the new culture may grow effete and it may be sought to re-illumine the altar fires from the primitive sources.

So men who constitute themselves the new priesthood of the New Age may seek for inspiration in the Bardic tradition once more. So you see the alternating generations of Bard and Priest. It follows from this that accurate scholarship in the historical sense cannot exist in such matters and the true scholarship is psychological which shall enable you to separate the primitive, which is valuable, from the literary and moralistic which is valueless and misleading. The *basic* sources of the Arthurian and Grail stories are pre-Christian, Bardic, to be sought in the primitive Keltic religion. The literary and moralistic influences which worked over the primitive story are to be sought in mediaeval religious thought and the Troubadour viewpoint.

Mediaeval religious thought confuses the issue by obliterating the traces of the primitive impulses and view-point of mankind and moralising the subject matter. But the Trouvères have the same view-point as the Bards for they developed their culture in the land where the influences of the Old Gods lived on, the southern part of France, home of the Albigenses. The Albigenses owed much to the same source. A great Mystery cult centred around Mont Segur, the background of the Trouvère, the secret cult of Queen Venus; and without understanding that, you will not understand the Arthurian romantic tales.

II.

The Arthurian tradition falls into two divisions: the Round Table stories and the Grail stories, but they are woven together by later annalists by the concept of the Quest. The knightly quests, which concern adventures with elemental forces, are elaborated into the spiritual quest of the Grail, and the Grail is restored to its place in the custody of women.

The Round Table formula concerns elemental forces, and the Grail formula concerns spiritual forces, and these form the Lesser and the Greater Mysteries of the Arthurian tradition. Look for the basic roots of the tradition in Druidical influences; seek its finest flower in mystical Christianity. And remember that in the background is the secret cult of Queen Venus.

So you have those three factors: the Druidical, the Witch-cult and Christian mysticism. The Druidical is a Nature-cult, sun-worship, the northern cult. The worship of Queen Venus, the Mediterranean or southern cult, derives its inspiration from the remains of the Roman culture, which derived from Greek sources primarily, with secondary tributaries from Mithraic and Persian sources. And the Greek tradition owed a very great deal to the Egyptian; and the Egyptian, in a later and debased form, influenced Roman thought.

Those are your factors in the Arthurian tradition, and scholarship is needed to determine the varying degrees of their influence in any given form of a legend. The early forms are naturally the most valuable because they are nearest to Druidical influences. But the Trouvère forms are also valuable because the Trouvères were initiates of the cult of Queen Venus and as such they understood the Bardic viewpoint.

The Trouvères and the Troubadours represented the esoteric and exoteric aspects of that brief flowering of Mediterranean culture that was stamped out in the Albigensian persecution. You will need to be on your guard in dealing with legends which are given specifically Christian form of the Roman communion as distinguished from the mystical Christian form of the Keltic tradition, and you can tell these apart quite readily: where the exponent of the Christian viewpoint is a priest, a monk or a nun, you are dealing with the roman influence; where the exponent is a hermit or anchorite you are dealing with the primitive Keltic influence.

Those are the lines that scholarship should pursue in relation to the Arthurian myth; it refers to the history of the early ages. The Roman civilisation was a conquering, military civilisation; the Greek was a civilisation of the mind and its influence was intellectual. The Greek culture, which is the basis of European culture, derived from several sources. It was first influenced by its own archaic tradition that lingered on in the islands and highlands of Greece when the cities became sophisticated, but this primitive religion, like all primitive religions, was a fertility cult of crops, herds and human beings. Then came the development of the state religion of the Olympian deities, and the Old Gods were forgotten. A later age outgrew the State religion, and turned to Egypt and Persia for the inspiration of their Mysteries. Persia derived her Mysteries from India and Chaldea. Egypt derived from Atlantis, and the influence of Egypt reached even to India. So may we trace the root source of all to Atlantis via Egypt and the Far and Near East, and also to those sacred islands in the North Sea and the north-western coasts of Europe where Atlantean influence penetrated. The Druidical Mysteries derive direct from Atlantis, as do the Egyptian; and the Greek Mystery cults drew their inspiration from Egypt and Persia (the priestly influence) and used the ancient material of the traditions lingering in the folk tales of the highlands and Islands of Greece as their symbolic texture, (the Bardic influence).

Rome drew her civilisation originally from Greek influences, and when she became sophisticated, drew on the Mystery cults of Greece, Persia and Egypt. And these cults, as well as the State religion, travelled with the legions, and wherever Roman troops settled down in occupation, Mystery schools were established.

The Roman policy was to assimilate the barbarian, and leading men of the local tribes were encouraged to send their sons to Rome to be educated. Very often they were taken as hostages when they were children, and given a Roman education, and then sent back to their tribes to rule under the tutelage of Rome. So Roman civilisation became naturalised in the conquered provinces.

The Mystery cults, being derived from primitive sources, presented no difficulties to the people of the conquered provinces, who had been nurtured in a similar tradition, and they were readily identified by them as their familiar deities. So the Mystery cults took hold and flourished, and when the Roman legions were rolled back by the Barbarian hordes, the Mystery cults lived on, having struck root in the soil. These persisted as a Pagan, or as later termed, a witch-cult tradition that still persists in the folk-lore of remote parts where the civilising influences of the centres of culture have not penetrated.

It was on these sources that the Trouvères drew. Now the Trouvères and the Troubadours and the Cathari and the Albigenses all developed their thought and systems under an impulse of intellectual activity which defied Catholicism and Christianity and formed part of the great heretical movements that were stamped out by persecution. And the Trouvères, who represented the Pagan mysticism of that movement, developed a cult of Mystery schools based on the ancient traditions of the Old Mysteries brought to that land by the Roman legions, who derived them from the Greek and Egyptian Mysteries. This Bardic tradition of the Trouvères recognising cognate material in the Druidical tradition of the Arthurian stories, made use of them in the same way as the Egyptian-initiated Greek mysteries drew on the primitive Greek Nature-cult for the myths which gave the formulae of the Eleusinian mysteries.

The Druidical form of the Arthurian tradition profoundly influenced the Keltic Christianity that developed in these islands. So we may say then, that the true Arthurian tradition is to be sought in the Druidical, the Keltic Christian, and the Trouvère sources, which know nothing of priesthood or monasteries or nunneries, but are familiar with hermits and holy pilgrims.

The hermit, the pilgrim, the magician and the Faery woman – these characterise the true tradition; and the priest, monastic organisation and the witch characterise the sophisticated mediaeval or Renaissance glosses on the primitive tradition, which are to be discarded as misleading. For instance, King Arthur being taken in death by the Faery women is primitive material and as such psychologically valid; Lancelot and Guinevere repenting them of their sins in their respective religious communities are later glosses, and as such, to be discarded from the Mystery tradition. You now see how and where to trace your sources.

At the back of the Trouvère recension of the Arthurian myth was the Queen Venus cult which kept secret, and later developed into the witch-cult, which contained features not recorded by the historians; and there was a highly developed cult of the women which showed itself clearly in Trouvère and Troubadour literature and in the Courts of Love, but which was discreetly ignored by the worthy Malory. Chrétien used Trouvère material and had more insight.

Ashtoreth was the fore-runner of Queen Venus and Guinevere was her successor; the records have been deliberately expunged. So we take their bones, in this valley of dead bones, and clothe them with the Mysteries, so that bone cleaves to bone and they become alive again.

> *March 1943 – In another attempt to assassinate Hitler, a bomb planted by German army officers on a plane carrying Hitler failed to go off.*

The foundations now start to be laid for the work of the Fraternity in the post-war period. A new Study Course is announced for those who aspire to membership, together with an appeal for financial support to aid the expanding venture. The weekly open meditation group has now ceased, and despite some requests that it be continued in some form, the focus of the group is now moving inward and the future lies with the training of dedicated initiates. Nonetheless in the sixth Monthly Letter Dion Fortune takes some pains to spell out the way for any who seek to make their first steps upon the path. The door is not closed even if it is no longer held wide open.

MONTHLY LETTER 6
for March 1943

EQUINOX APPEAL

The Vernal Equinox comes round once more, and we must make our biannual appeal for financial support to those who consider our work of sufficient value to be maintained in being through the difficult days of the war, when there is little opportunity for personal participation for most people.

Our friends have been more than good in the support they have afforded us, and we hope and believe that this will be continued. As with everyone else, our expenses are rising and our income falling. It is only because of a member who, during the past year having received an unexpected windfall of capital, has most generously passed on the benefit to the Fraternity, that we have been able to remain solvent, and we cannot expect this to happen a second time.

Either we must find ways to increase our income or the falling financial tide will sooner or later leave us stranded. We should welcome suggestions from the friends of the Fraternity as well as its members. We should also welcome suggestions for developments in our work. Recently we have had letters from more than one person asking for a renewal of the meditation work by the setting of meditation subjects for the month in the pages of this Letter.

An effectual meditation group could not be formed in this way. It must have as its nucleus a group of people who sit in circle formation with someone trained in meditation as the leader. We should be glad to know whether there are any among our friends and members who would be prepared to join such a group if it were formed, also what hour and day would be considered most convenient? If the scheme proves feasible, we will arrange for such a group to meet in the Library at our Headquarters, and for instruction papers to be got out concerning the method to be used by those working at a distance.

In spite of wartime conditions, we are steadily adding to the library by the purchase and the gift of books. We have good facilities for exchanging duplicates, or selling advantageously books unsuitable for our shelves, and we hope our friends will give the library their support both as borrowers and donors so that it may be the better equipped for its useful work. So far as we know, there is no other occult library in the country that gets the new books as we do.

THE NEW STUDY COURSE

It is not possible for many people to pursue the studies and submit to the discipline of the training that leads to initiation, yet nevertheless much useful work could be done by sincerely dedicated persons, and esoteric schools, like industry, must be prepared to organise the energies of part time workers. We have therefore devised an initial training course that shall enable people to co-operate with the Mystery Tradition without the necessity of actually taking initiation. Those who desire to do so can, of course, go on to further training; but there is a wide field of useful work that can be done in the Outer Court by those who are sincere in their desire to serve, provided they can grasp the main ideas and are prepared to go to work systematically.

The Mystery Tradition has often been likened to an iceberg, of which but a small proportion is above the surface and the great mass out of sight. But a small part of an esoteric Order exists on the Physical Plane; all the greater and more important aspects are on the Inner Planes. The mundane aspect of an Order is practically nothing but a training school wherein mind training is done – a mind training designed to serve spiritual ends, for schools of the Right Hand Path are most careful that their training shall never be used for ends of personal power and aggrandizement. Those who are fully trained learn to use the channel of communication with the Inner Planes both for the receiving of teaching and instruction and the bringing through of that concentrated form of spiritual force that enables the service of God and man to be performed with power. It is obvious that such work can only be entrusted to carefully chosen and trained persons, but we found in the days when we threw open our doors during the Siege of London that the tensions of war had brought spiritual growth to the nation en masse, and that a very great many people were ready and able to co-operate in the work of the Mystery Tradition.

In order to do this, they have, first and foremost, to get into touch with the Tradition on the Inner Planes, so that they become, in the language of the Mysteries, 'on their contacts', without which no work can be done. Getting into touch with the Mysteries depends on two things: knowing where to look, and the right approach. Knowing where to look depends on right information; the right approach depends on the right kind of character, and this is a character that has a selfless desire to serve and a willingness to observe discipline. The desire to serve by itself is not enough – the road to Hell is proverbially paved with good intentions – because work in connection with an esoteric Order involves co-operation with others, both on the Physical Plane and on the Inner Planes, and unless people are prepared to observe some sort of simple rule, such co-operation is impossible. The aim of the organisation of an order or Fraternity is to render co-operation possible between the physical plane and the Inner Planes. The Spiritualist Movement demonstrates the possibility of communication, but it is the Mystery Tradition that practises co-operation.

Granted the right kind of character, it is only necessary to indicate where to look in order that the search may be rewarded; for those who approach in the right spirit carry the key in their hands. The place in which to look for the Mystery Tradition is on the Inner Planes. We turn inward, into the Silence, to make our contacts, not to any spot on the physical earth. The contact with the Masters on the Inner Planes is made by thinking about them. The pictorial imagination is one of the principle instruments used in esoteric work, and by careful training and constant practice it is brought to a very fine edge. In consequence, it is possible to build up very clear cut and detailed mental images. These images are, in reality, astral thought forms, and they are the channels through which the invisible forces work. In order to enable the imagination to get to function, it has to be provided with material, just as a novelist who wanted to write an historical novel would study the period in which he proposed to lay his scene until he could picture it in all its detail of dress, architecture and customs.

Most of the students who enrolled in our study courses in the past already knew a good deal about esoteric science when they came to us. We have always been teachers of teachers, training in the high ranges of knowledge people who were already experienced in occult studies. Consequently there was in our study courses little that the beginner could make a start upon. We had no propaganda. Students who came to us had to pick up our trail on the Inner Planes; consequently they had to have at least some natural aptitude and a certain amount of knowledge before they made contact. In fact we found that, almost without exception they had been initiates of the Tradition in past lives, and we come to look upon this as a *sine qua non* of initiation into our Fraternity.

But with the opening of the gates it becomes necessary to enable people to 'start from cold' as it were. In order to do this, we have devised an entirely new study course, which consists in the reading and discussion of my two little books, *Esoteric Orders and Their Work* and *The Training and Work of an Initiate*. These books give a general concept of the Mystery Tradition and its workings and the student who has read them, and thought about them, especially the latter, can, if he has the right kind of character, pick up his contacts with the Mystery Tradition on the Inner Planes. Or to be more precise, the Tradition will pick him up. To discuss the ideas contained in these books under the direction of a teacher or group leader is the best way of getting into contact with the Tradition, but where personal presence is impossible, we are arranging for students to correspond with members of our Fraternity and so make a personal contact, even if an indirect one. We are not asking those who join our Initial Training Course to pass examinations, but only to think about, and either write or talk about, the ideas in these two little books.

This may seem very simple and unexacting, but it is not quite as haphazard as it looks, for unless there is the 'right approach', nothing will happen. But those who bring to the altar of the Mysteries acceptable gifts of character and dedication will, sooner or later, and more often sooner than later, find that in a sudden flash of reality the Masters have made contact. Such a flash is usually a brief moment of illumination; it is impossible to hold it for longer than that in any intensity; it may, in a less intense form, or as the aftermath of such a moment, continue for some days as a state of spiritual insight and exaltation, but it never by any chance continues long. If it did, it would disorganise the mind by its intensity, for the untrained human mind is not built to carry such voltages, hence the prolonged training that is necessary in order to attain to the higher grades of initiation. But some sudden sense of reality there can and should be as a result of study along the lines indicated. It may be as faint and elusive as the fragrance of flowers in the dark; but it will nevertheless be something outside the ordinary range of experience and it will convey the sense that the Invisible Realities are real – that they have been known at first hand, and that one is no longer dependent upon second hand testimony for knowledge of the Secret Wisdom and all that proceeds from it.

Once this flash of reality has come – and gone – the student is in an entirely different position, for he has been 'contacted'. Whatever doubts and difficulties may fall to his lot in the future, he will never lose his sense of reality of an invisible world which is the Plane of Causation to our world. He can, moreover, put the matter to the test experimentally. If at a time when his consciousness is heightened by spiritual tension in difficulty or danger he reconstructs in his imagination the scene of his exaltation and involves the Master who then contacted him, that Master will come through again and in some way make his presence known. Sometimes it is done by a renewal of that same inner sense of reality; sometimes by definite physical signs such as a sense of glowing heat, the movement of air in a still room, the scent of flowers or incense, a bell-like note, or even, to those who are naturally psychic, the actual Presence manifesting. Those who follow the Mystery Tradition do not need to depend upon second hand evidence. Ours is not a school which teaches a doctrine only. Unless we can give first hand experience we consider we have failed to initiate.

Now as to the work that can be done by those who take the Initial Training and serve in the Outer Court. Each day for a quarter of an hour they are asked to sit quietly in meditation, thinking of the Masters and their work for humanity. As the concept becomes clear to them and they 'get on to their contacts', they become like radio transmitters through which the influence of the Masters comes through to humanity for the healing of the nations.

April 1943 – On the orders of Himmler, after strong resistance, SS troops finally kill or transport 60,000 Jews from the Warsaw Ghetto.

In the seventh Monthly Letter Dion Fortune turns to the type of work with which initiates of a modern esoteric fraternity should be concerned. There are two aspects to this. One is a teaching role, the other the practical use of what is learned in the teaching. This implies the use of powers of the mind and their possible abuse, although as Dion Fortune points out, this is by no means a problem exclusive to esoteric fraternities. In these, the principle safeguard is the quality and direction of the initiate's dedication, and the oversight of the Masters in a properly contacted group.

MONTHLY LETTER 7
for April 1943

THE WORK OF THE INITIATE IN THE WORLD OF TODAY

Those who look back through the files of the Weekly Letters will note a distinct difference in subject matter between them and their successors, the Monthly Letters. The Weekly Letters dealt with day to day topics during the critical early phases of the war, when our morale needed all the help it could get and the incoming life wave had not yet been canalised into its appointed course. A new energy was surging into the soul of the nation as it roused itself to fight for its life, and those of us who looked out upon the scene from the Watch Tower on the Hill of Vision knew that unless this energy were directed to ends beyond the immediate war aims it would sink into the sands of time once more for lack of a defined channel.

Therefore although our organisation is definitely non-political, we felt that we could not do otherwise than indicate the significance of the things that were happening in the soul of the nation because it is only the mystical psychologist who has any inkling as to what they are; and although there are many mystics and still more psychologists, outside our ranks we doubt if there are many, or even any, mystical psychologists; so it had to be us or nobody. We had several resignations from old members who were displeased because we expressed the opinion that things would, and should, change profoundly, but we had a great many more admissions of new members who felt that we could give them the particular kind of inner light they needed.

In due course we felt that we had covered the ground that needed covering; and we saw that, as we had been promised, those who could command the attention of the nation were giving direction and organisation to the ideals which we could only formulate and intellectualise. We therefore felt that our work in this direction was done, and so we changed the Weekly Letters into a monthly communication which permitted of longer and more varied articles; and putting aside the day to day comments on a situation which no longer possessed the same urgency, we once again directed our attention to 'pure' as distinguished from 'applied' esoteric science.

But as those who have studied the 'Tree of Life' know, the swing of the pendulum is inherent in evolution, and once again we must turn our attention, though not exclusively, to mundane problems; not by descending into the political arena, but by making the particular contribution to the mental life of our race which it is in our power, and in that of none other, to make.

This contribution takes two forms. Its primary form consists in explaining the esoteric knowledge concerning evolution and human nature and destiny, and in showing the practical application of those doctrines to the problems of human life, individual and collective. On the basis of the principles that clearly emerge from the esoteric teachings it will be found possible to work out a broad scheme of reconstruction for society and of a way of life for individuals that shall be no patchwork of expediencies, no short-term policy of opportunism, but a plan that shall be based on, and co-ordinated with, the vast evolutionary movement which is the Will of God.

Only what is built on such lines can endure; all else must inevitably fall as the evolutionary tide rises, and, before its final disintegration, cause untold suffering because it is 'against nature'. The better the organisation and the more powerful the interests that support it, the greater the suffering and confusion if the original plan be wrongly conceived. But however powerful and efficient it may be, it cannot endure indefinitely because "He shall turn and overturn till He whose right it is shall reign." But in addition to this, the primary educational aspect of our work, there is another aspect which cannot rightly be called secondary to the first because without the contribution it has to make, the primary purpose may well be rendered inoperative. It is secondary in the time sense only, in that the primary work of understanding cosmic principles must come first, for without such knowledge taken to heart, the supplementary aspects are both incomprehensible and dangerous. This is not a contradiction in terms, for it is possible to understand enough of the teaching to make a rule of thumb application of it without any realisation of the principles on which it rests and in the light of which only it can be properly applied.

This secondary teaching is a part of the secret teaching of the Mysteries, carefully guarded by those to whom it has been entrusted because of its immense power for evil as well as for good. In the right hands it is for the healing of the nations and the initiation of individuals; in the wrong hands it affords a ready means of reducing both nations and individuals to slavery.

It has been widely used for this purpose of recent years, and is regarded as a practical application of psychology or mind power. There are innumerable correspondence courses, mostly American in origin, based on half-understood applications of the great principles of creative mind power. They owe their origin in the first place to the revelation of the power of the mind and its practical application given by Mrs Eddy in Christian Science, and she, although it is denied in the orthodox accounts of her life, can be clearly proven to have derived her ideas in the first place from Quimby the hypnotist. She was, however, fully alive to the fact that the powers she developed had a dark side as well as a divine one, and took every precaution she could think of to prevent this dark side from being exploited. To this end she drew a sharp distinction between what she called the Divine Mind and 'mortal mind, or the mind of mortals'. Critically examined, this distinction will not hold water; for man has but one mind with which to serve good or evil; but the distinction served a purpose in preventing the unsophisticated from experimenting along undesirable lines, and enabled them to get the maximum good out of the directed use of mind power and reduced its abuse to a minimum. Her device did not succeed, however, in deceiving the discerning, and out of a realisation of what the mind could do when purposefully directed, arose a flock of schools and correspondence courses for the development of 'personality' in the service of salesmanship, sex attraction and domination over others – all logical if not legitimate developments of Mrs Eddy's teaching, and against which nothing could guard once the well kept secret of the Mysteries was 'out'. It was for this reason that such knowledge has been kept secret by the initiates who are its repositories. Now it is out, however, it has got to be reckoned with, and the only way it can be dealt with is by understanding it thoroughly and developing the antidote.

We now find ourselves in the same dilemma that confronted Mrs Eddy – if we give out the knowledge necessary to combat the abuse of mind power, we supply the enemies of mankind with additional weapons, for mind power is a means to many ends and can be used indifferently for good or evil according to its motivation and direction. We therefore propose to pursue, for the present at any rate, a midway course, and to tell enough to enable the operations of mind power to be recognised, but not enough to enable the uninitiated to know how it is done. This affords a medium of negative protection in that it enables people to be on their guard and prevents them from being taken unawares and got under control by insidious means. We can go further than this, and supply certain formulae of protection which are of great value; but we dare not go the whole way and teach openly the real esoteric methods of mind-working lest these led to worse evils than the ones they seek to combat.

Nevertheless, it is urgently necessary to combat the organised forces abroad in the world, and for this purpose the deeper knowledge is necessary. But in giving this we shall abide by the tradition of the Mysteries in restricting it to those who have proved themselves worthy to be entrusted with it and have undergone the discipline necessary to enable them to make practical application of the secret philosophy.

The original development of the dark side of the Secret Wisdom is to be sought in the various mind power training courses so widely developed in the United States. Similar courses here are, as far as I know, for the most part importations of, or adaptions from, the original American sources. The English variety is more scrupulous in its methods and less extreme in its commercialism than the American, but though advertised as correspondence courses and charged for at a price which would be expected to include tuition, the amount of personal attention given to students is usually negligible and bears no relationship to the fees demanded. The courses might just as well have been published in book form at shillings instead of guineas, and with very few honourable exceptions, the whole correspondence course ramp written off as a catchpenny device.

The application of psychology to salesmanship did not stop at the cultivation of the personality of the salesman, however, but went on to study of the use of mental suggestion by means of advertisement. This has been worked out with great skill in the drink trade, wherein a realistic picture of an overflowing glass and a slogan concerning its medicinal nature are widely used. The suggestion of a health value supplies an excuse, and the sight of the overflowing glass awakens desire. The path of an inebriate striving to overcome his craving is made infinitely harder by such pictorial publicity, and it ought to be prohibited for the same reason that pornography is prohibited. Other examples of such trading in human weakness are those which exploit snobbery in the cause of soap, less harmful no doubt, but equally illegitimate in principle.

Out of advertising psychology came the next step – the use of mass suggestibility for political purpose. The methods of revivalist religion and political spell-binders had long been identical, and so to say that it is not necessarily to condemn either or both, for it is only by such methods that the masses can be approached. Like other forms of mind power, they are not good or evil in themselves, but only in the use to which they are put. 'Billy Brown of London Town' with his lyrical advice on behaviour in buses, so much more effective than the crude command 'Do not spit' is an example of the right use of mass appeal. His humorous admonitions are accepted without the resentment that is aroused by commands and the association of delinquency with half-wittedness so admirably conveyed by the pictures robs law-breaking of its charm, and the horror and disgust depicted on the faces of the onlookers at evil doings makes the best use of the snobbery that is innate in all save the nihilist, who may be trusted not to misbehave in buses anyway.

Early in the history of broadcasting its propaganda value was appreciated. In this country it was kept under government control and rigidly guarded against exploitation and abuse. In America its advertising value has been exploited, to the boredom of listeners, but on the whole it has not been basely used, unless the religious broadcasts of fantasies be considered an abuse, as well they may be when they instil fear or hatred. In Germany, however, it has been a different story. All that is known of mass suggestion has been placed at the service of Totalitarian ideology and ruthlessly exploited; and along with such Totalitarian use of propaganda goes the concomitant of the repression of all competing viewpoints that might serve as a starting point for rival propaganda. If you once start to influence or control minds, it is very difficult to know where you can end, or where the lines between legitimate guidance and undue influence can rightly be drawn. Very great wisdom and scrupulousness are needed for the right use of mental power. It is so insidious that it can be used unobserved, and therefore public opinion affords no safeguard. It is also liable to give rise to a sense of omnipotence and omniscience in those who use it that can only be kept in check by a deep sense of dedication, complete integrity and sincere humility, and this is to ask a great deal of any human being.

There is only one efficient safeguard for the use of the powers conferred by a knowledge of the Secret Wisdom, and that is the discipline imposed on the initiate of the Mysteries by the fact that he is answerable to the Masters from whom no secret is hid, not even the secrets below the level of consciousness. The initiate who uses mind power does so under very strict safeguards. He can never develop any sense of omnipotence and omniscience because he knows that his work is only a part of a plan as vast as the universe, and that he has to fit in with fellow workers serving God and man in a planned scheme. He himself is never the planner. There is but one Planner, and that is the Cosmic Mind. The task of the initiate, dedicated to the service of God and man, is to wait upon the Will of God in the silence until it becomes clear to him. He will then find that he has a certain definitely circumscribed part to play in a vast co-ordination of activities, and that before he can even play the small part assigned to him, he must prepare himself for it by rigorous self-discipline. His first task will be to make good as a human being in whatever sphere to which it has pleased God to call him, for no one is entrusted with cosmic tasks until he has proved himself upon mundane ones. It is never to the ineffective, unco-ordinated, or the ambitious that such responsibilities are entrusted. The power to influence other people is only entrusted to persons who have no desire whatever to use it, who have, in fact, a distaste for the task because they realise the terrible responsibilities involved. The greatest powers are always wielded in obscurity by initiates of the Hermetic type who have nothing to gain by success and no means of reaping the fruits of their labours or taste for enjoying them.

Promotion from grade to grade of the Mysteries does not involve eminence, but greater obscurity and austerity. Those who travel on the path, travel light. It is also a law of the Mysteries that no one can take a higher grade until he has trained his successor and handed over his task to him. Thus, far from guarding jealously the Secret Wisdom, initiates are always anxiously seeking for suitable successors in order that they may be free to take their grades, and the higher the grade, the harder are such to find.

Under such conditions, and especially because each worker is entrusted with a strictly circumscribed task, the abuse of power by initiates is difficult and rare; and because the masters on the Inner Planes who direct the work can see the soul as clearly as we see the body, any aberration is quickly detected and dealt with by cutting the offender off from the cosmic scheme and turning him loose to deal as best he may with the forces he has set in motion. This is sufficient punishment for any man.

January 1944 – 50,000 Allied troops land at Anzio in Italy. In Russia, the Red Army breaks the 872 day seige of Leningrad.

The Monthly Letters that follow contain a number of long serial articles, such as "The Principles of Hermetic Philosophy". These have since been published in a series of volumes by Thoth Publications, and this serialisation in Fraternity papers is a time honoured way in which Dion Fortune wrote most of her books. However, shorter articles still found a place, as this one, in which she reiterates her belief in the importance of there being three strands in the discipline of the Mysteries. She describes them as devotional, intellectual and artistic, which might be put in another way as the way of the mystic, the magician and the shaman. The ideal is the initiate who is at home in all three.

She also sees the dawning of a New Age in terms contemporary to her own viewpoint, with the Piscean Age going out with the First World War, the Aquarian Age coming in at the end of the Second World War, with the 'cusp' between the two in the inter-war period. If not strictly in accordance with the astronomical indicators it at least had the pragmatic quality of concentrating her mind on what she sought to achieve. And her concluding remarks demonstrate that she certainly knew all about the 'hands on' reality of running a magical fraternity. As she was so fond of saying: "an ounce of practice is worth a pound of theory!"

MONTHLY LETTER 14
for January 1944

CONCERNING THE DIVERSITY OF GIFTS

In a Fraternity making use of ceremonial and various forms of group working, it is necessary that a fraternal spirit in the fullest and highest sense of the word should prevail. The group mind becomes closely knit, and any rift between individual members affects the integration of the whole and disturbs, or if sufficiently severe, prevents magical working. The brethren will recall occasions when it has been necessary to cancel lodges for no other reason than a disturbed mental atmosphere within the group. Such close fellowship can only be maintained if there is the kind of tolerance among us that comes from an imaginative insight which enables people to understand and appreciate a mode of approach or method of working which they themselves do not share or are temperamentally incapable of achieving. This is very far removed from what is ordinarily understood by tolerance, which always seemed to imply something of contempt only kept within bounds by lack of power to give it expression in persecution. We tolerate what we cannot stop. The tolerance that should prevail in the Mysteries is better characterised by such terms as broad-mindedness and generosity, the willingness to admit that it is possible that we ourselves might be mistaken, or that what we have received from authoritative sources that seemed to us unquestionable might be outmoded by the passage of time and require modification; and that there is more than one kind of excellence in the world. In other words, "There is diversity of gifts, but the same spirit."

Our Fraternity makes provision for three main types of temperament, the devotional, the intellectual, and the artistic; consequently there is wide divergence of type among its members, and this diversity we encourage, considering it wholesome as leading to balance and broad-mindedness. There are profound truths in the terse and witty lines we would do so well to remember:

"If all the good people were clever,
And all clever people were good,
The world would be better than ever
We thought it possibly could.

But alas, it is seldom or never
That matters turn out as they should –
The good are so hard on the clever,
And the clever so rude to the good."

But amid all the diversity we can distinguish a definite classification, and an appreciation of this may make it easier for the brethren to understand each other. This classification, as no student of the Qabalah needs to be told, follows the lines of the Tree of Life. There are the three main types as previously indicated, just as there are the three Pillars upon the

Tree; and there are different planes upon each pillar. The pillars traverse the Tree vertically, and the planes horizontally. But although we can distinguish three basic temperaments following three distinct paths in theory, in actual practice we find few pure ray types, for people invariably contain all three aspects in their natures in differing proportions, and it is the percentage of proportion that determines their primary Ray. Nevertheless, there are few among us who are content to work on one Ray only, few who are content to be purely devotional with no tincture of the Hermetic Wisdom, for instance. Equally, however, there are few who can combine all three modes of ray working. A primary and secondary ray working is practically universal among our members; so even though the balanced triangle is rare, there should always be some aspect of all that can be touched by each, and none should be entirely out of range of sympathy of any. If this occurs, something goes wrong with the group aura, and the rift soon declares itself and requires to be dealt with. We deal with it by excision. However excellent they may be as individuals, one or both have to go for the good of the Fraternity if they cannot keep the peace. In magical working, the keeping of the peace consists of more than the absence of any overt breach of civility; it consists in that inner harmony and goodwill which is the microcosmic equivalent of the music of the spheres.

The problem of type harmonisation in our Fraternity is further complicated by the time factor. Our work began at the close of the Piscean Age and was carried out by advanced Visceans, pioneering the new ideas that were beginning to unfold in the racial consciousness. Time went by; evolution moved on; the purely Piscean Age passed away with the First World War, and we entered upon the cusp, or transition stage between Ages. The main work of the Fraternity was then carried on by people of the cusp, and the two types, the pure Piscean and the cusp Piscean, had to fit in together as best they might. There were difficulties, some of which were only solved by resignations.

Then, with the Second World War, we began to pass out of the cusp phase, and pure Aquarian types made their appearance among us. All through the cusp phase I, as Warden, held the Fraternity together ruthlessly, modifying nothing and placating no one, and letting who would resign, taking their subscriptions with them. I have always been particularly careful to allow no one to obtain such a position of influence in the Fraternity, for any reason, financial or other, that they could bring about a preponderance of the ray they favoured. This has sometimes pressed hardly on individuals, who, having given long and loyal services and made great sacrifices, felt they were entitled to consideration. This they never got, and never will get. The Masters never accept gifts with strings tied to them. What is given, is given; and once accepted, passes out of the Donor's control, to be used in the service of the policy of the Fraternity as directed by the Masters. All voting is by a show of hands, or if controversial, by ballot, not by the equivalent of a share-holding in the Fraternity's spiritual stock. All souls are sacred, but none are privileged. By neither gifts nor services can anyone buy anything save opportunity in the Fraternity. What use they make of the opportunity thus afforded them depends on nothing but their own capacity. The Masters accept what is given in a spirit of dedication, which means that the giving must be selfless and without ulterior motive. Many have given their all, myself among them; but I think I can justly say that no one has taken such risks as I have run in the service of the Masters. Every new development of magical work involves risk until it is well established and in working order. I select certain persons to help me with the pioneering, and they undergo definite risk should anything go wrong with the working; but as leader I am the first to venture out into the Unknown, and if the psychic ice will not bear, I am the one to go through. If anything goes wrong, I have to see everybody safely back before I can make my own escape. If the power gets out of hand, I have to earth it if I can, and if I failed, I should play the part of the blown fuse in an electrical installation. We do not always succeed at the first attempt in establishing a new grade on a Ray, and each failure involves a critically dangerous moment as we who are concerned get out from under the falling structure. The brethren of the rank and file see the finished work, the smoothly flowing force, but unless something goes wrong, they have little realisation of what a head of power there is in the working. It is so smooth it appears effortless; but it is only effortless because it is expert.

March 1944 – In an attempt break the deadlock at Monte Cassino, the Allies blanket bomb the town with 775 aircraft and 1750 tons of bombs. The town is being held by 350 German troops.

In the seventh Monthly Letter Dion Fortune had put forward her belief that dedication to the Masters was the safeguard against the abuse of occult power. Some might say that this presupposes choosing the right Master. No doubt this is why, in the tradition taught by the fraternity, the two first tests for the seeker upon the path were held to be 'discretion' and 'discrimination'. In other words, the ability to discern the true and the good before giving allegiance to what might only pass for it. For this reason the publication of the "Words of the Masters" papers had a dual purpose. They served not only as lectures for the teaching of esoteric principles but by their tone and inherent power enabled an answering chord to be struck within the soul of the neophyte who was likely to be ready for them. The following example illustrates this principle very well.

MONTHLY LETTER 16
for March 1944

WORDS OF THE MASTERS

Seek first the Master on the Inner Planes, and when the time is ripe he will bring you to the initiator who is his servant. The Master on the Inner Planes trains the subjective consciousness, but it requires the mediation of the initiator to train the objective consciousness and to unite the two, so that the objective can be subjective and subjective objective. This is the meaning of the "open eyes" in the phase of Enlightenment.

Wisdom, Strength and Love came in the order of manifestation. Wisdom came first and gave rise to Strength. Strength came next and gave rise to Love. There is no love without Strength. Love also has a wisdom of its own, and Love, Wisdom and Power are needed in the Mysteries. Uphold the ideal, for if it be lifted up it must, by its very beauty and truth draw all men unto it; and ye can draw where ye cannot persuade. The Masters need those who can stand up before them and before the world, and interpret them to the world by speech and by their lives.

Always bear in mind that devotion is the crown of the whole edifice; that we are all manifestations of the Divine Life – part of God, and all our actions and aims should ever bear relation to that fact; that our mundane manifestation is the projection down the planes of the consciousness of the Logos. That God grows through us. That by our actions we help or hinder the progress of God; our existence has its own origin in God. All must be lived in relation to God, for we are part of God. This is the worship of God the Father which is the highest worship of all. The worship of God the Son as Redeemer and Master concerns the personality and, therefore, is the Most Holy called Lord of the Body. The worship of the Third Person of the Trinity concerns the individuality – the higher consciousness, and it is His power which initiates. He is the Great Initiator. The Father is the

Creator and Sustainer in Whom and of Whom are all things. The Son is the projection into matter of the Divine Power in form. The Holy Spirit is the power in manifestation.

It is the aim to bring all to attainment if it be in any wise possible. So bear you one another's burdens, and remember that you can always take your problems to the Master and ask for wisdom and strength. It is to be had for the asking. The only people we do not help are those who do not realise their need – those who say: "Drive the lion from my path," and do not see that it is their own shadow thrown ahead of them. For if there is a beast of prey in the heart, it will cast a shadow of a lion on the path.

To each man according to his aura. We weigh the effort as well as the achievement, but do not forget to weigh the achievement as well as the effort. Learn to know failure when you see it and to find out the reasons thereof. For thereby you draw the power out of failure and absorb it. We never discard any soul.

The constant demands of the mundane world draw away from the Unseen. While the material activities are very necessary while contacts are being established, they are better set aside after the work commences. They tend to objectify the consciousness too much and prevent the necessary in-turning. Where the mind is, there will the consciousness be; and when the mind is centred upon the cares of the mundane world, the unseen world recedes. It is not possible to be with Mary and with Martha When Mary sat at the feet of Her Lord, she neglected her household tasks, and although the household tasks are essential, Martha while performing them, could not sit at the feet of Her Lord. Martha was upon the Path of the Server. Mary, having passed the tests of the dedicand, had had her dedication accepted and was approaching the state of Enlightenment. She, therefore, left the household tasks to Martha, and quite rightly.

There must be no sense of separateness in those who are upon the Path, for the Path has its goal in the great Unity wherein all are One and One is all. Whatever is evil in the world – whatever is partial or limited – imperfect or distorted, is a part of yourself, and you suffer with its failures and triumph with its achievements. Those who dedicate themselves to service can separate themselves from nothing, but become merged in the world as it is, in order that they may dilute it with spirit. And remember that having dedicated yourself, you belong primarily to your Master and that his claim is the paramount claim.

So live, so order your thoughts, so regulate your minds that the channel may be kept open, for the channel is needed.

Be not too bound to the wheel of life; you are called to higher service than the service of any person. Where there is a clash of duties, follow the higher duty. We give to those who ask. Be ready to follow greater paths. There is much you discern not, both of the greater and the less – of the personality and the individuality, for the individuality cannot play its part without the co-operation of the personality.

Through all difficulties and dangers the work must go on, calling upon the name of the Masters. And be assured of this – there can be no harm done in spite of the ebb, flow, storm and wreckage of what is personal. Trust the Masters upon the bigger issue.

Upon all sides will opposition flow in, but fear not. That which is eternal will overcome that which is temporal. Only those live who live in eternity.

You are gathered together for service, and we have given you certain things in order to enable you to serve. Personality ministers unto personality so that the individualities may be free for higher work. Let not the stress be thrown on the personality, but rather on the individuality.

There is always work for those who are willing to serve, but the work comes first and must be put first. We ask much of those who serve us, and when they give, we pay interest. We ask faith, not because we do not trust, but because you cannot understand.

Before we give you the work, we test you. It is better that the empty vessel should fall to pieces than the full one. We strike the vessel before we proceed to fill it. There are certain tests which, having been taken, open out new planes.

Learn that the Divine man upon the Seventh Plane permeates all things. Learn universal sympathy. Learn to identify yourself with the universe so that nothing shall seem alien to you. Learn to see the universe reflected in yourself and yourself in the universe. Is a nation sick – so are you. Is a city sinful – so are you. There is no crime or lust known to the history of the race that is not a potentially latent in your own nature. There is not a height to which humanity has risen which is not a potentially also latent in your own nature. No human being can divorce himself from either the depths or heights of his species.

Value in spiritual values, in states of consciousness. If so be you had all things and were sick, you could not eat; and were crippled, you could not wear rich raiment; and if you had all wealth and houses and had not God, the spirit of man within you would be athirst and, standing in the cornfield, would cry out upon the barren land; and if you had all knowledge and all books, and the eye of the spirit were shut; though you knew all wisdom, you would not know the import thereof; and having set before you the values of the spirit, you will receive the things of the spirit. Judge not results with the eye of man, but by the values of the land whereon thou dost live.

> April 1944 – In preparation for the forthcoming invasion, the Allies step up their bombing campaign in Europe. 75% of France's railways are now out of action.

Important issues in the deeper aspects of occultism are the dual factors of land and of blood. And it is perhaps because of their power and potential in terms of the group souls, group minds and group angels of nations that they so readily become the cause for conflict. As was said in another context by a much misunderstood initiate "for we wrestle not against flesh and blood but against principalities, against powers". It is not for nothing that this passage comes from a chapter in the Letter to the Ephesians devoted to giving honour to one's father and mother, the most immediate of one's ancestors, or that Principalities and Powers in the angelology of Dionysius the Areopagite, refer to those orders having concern with the nations. A deeper appreciation of the spiritual complexities of these matters might go some way to seeing a little further into the inner causes of seemingly intractable territorial, racial and religious conflict.

Dion Fortune has already made it plain in the Letters that she has no truck with religious or racial prejudice but nonetheless there are differences resulting from ancestry, land of birth and domicile that need to be taken into account in practical occultism. In the following article she draws some interesting lines of distinction in tracing the areas of spiritual jurisdiction over the varied territories of the British Isles and Western Europe. Another factor bearing upon all of this is the place of oriental teaching in the context of the western tradition.

MONTHLY LETTER 17
for April 1944

CONCERNING THE ORGANISATION AND METHOD OF DISCIPLINE IN THE WESTERN TRADITION

The distinction between East and West is more than a question of terminology, it concerns Jurisdiction. It is therefore necessary to define frankly and carefully what this term implies.

In the heights, all are one and one is all; descending down the planes, there is divergence of type owing to divergence of experience. This divergence is due to the fact that the Cosmic Rays swing into manifestation in rotation; consequently the phases of evolution issuing into manifestation receive their first impress of form under different Rays and are consequently different in primary type and so react differently to all subsequent experience. But because all souls have to experience all Rays in the course of their evolution, there is no ultimate difference or disunity, though temporary differences, leading to temporary disunity, must be reckoned with in all human calculations. The more evolved the soul, the more Rays he will have experienced, and therefore the wider his sympathies with divergent types because he has in him something of them all; the more lowly the soul, the more limited its sympathies because the more limited its experience.

Nevertheless, souls are organised by types while still in their earlier phases of development, and these types are called Group Souls and are rooted in the Earth; Group Minds, in contradistinction, depend on the development of cultures and bear no relationship to place. A Group Soul sets its ineradicable impress on a soul that has experienced incarnation therein, and a soul that has not had that experience lacks that impress and has no part in its life. Under exceptional conditions of high initiation, it is possible to make a soul free of another race, but this is rare, and only undertaken for an express purpose, e.g. the re-establishing of a lost culture; apart from this it is seldom either desirable or practicable, for a soul depends upon the Group Soul into which it incarnates for a portion of its subconscious background and basis, hence the problem of the crossbred.

Only in the higher ranges of evolution, wherein individualisation is achieved and the soul has drawn clear of its immersion in the Group Soul can these problems be solved. Below that level, they are best not attempted, and the instinct for racial purity is a sound one.

Because of these things, which are stated in explanation, racial types are guided in their destiny by Racial Angels and initiated by racial Masters. The Masters, however, are all brethren one of another, for at their level, there is no division into creed, caste or race. To each group of Masters there is committed a Jurisdiction.

Originally, racial and geographical Jurisdiction were one; but owing to the migrations of peoples, confusion and complication ensued, and periodically in the Earth's history there have been readjustments. There is neither occasion nor opportunity at the present moment to consider the past history of these things, interesting and valuable though they are, for we are concerned with practical matters and must adhere to the points that concern them.

The Western Tradition at the present time consists of those whose staple food is leavened bread, regardless of their geographical distribution, for the white race can only breed where wheat will flourish. The bread-eaters are again subdivided into the drinkers of wine, of beer, and of distilled spirits, corresponding to the Latin, the Norse and the Keltic races. But because the white races have spread far afield through conquest and emigration, and overflowed the boundaries of one another and of alien races, account must be taken of the Place-Soul as well as the Group Soul in calculating matters referring to racial contacts; for the Group Soul, being rooted in the Earth, acquires a Place aspect with the passage of time.

In the races inhabiting the British Isles we are confronted by a particularly intricate problem. Their collaterals are spread far over the earth's surface, yet retain their roots in the Motherland; and owing to the free intermingling of cultures, beer, wine and spirits are equally the drink of the islanders. Thus a unified Group Mind has grown up on the basis of a diversified Group Soul, and of this diversification of the Group Soul account must be taken in initiating. Furthermore, the custom of giving a classical education, thus making contact with Greek and Roman traditions, and giving this only to the males of the ruling caste, makes another line of cleavage.

Owing to this diversity within unity which yet retains sympathy, the Western Tradition in these islands is multiform, and though initiates may find one or another aspect the more congenial owing to past incarnations or present affiliations, all can and should enter freely into each. Of these there are three distinct lines – the Keltic, the Norse, and what can only be described as the Conglomerate, being that which is composed of all the different elements that have ever struck roots in British soil. The Keltic and the Norse are divided by a line drawn from the Holy Isle, off the coast of Northumbria, to St Alban's Head in Wessex. All who derive from the west of the line will have basically Keltic contacts in their deepest unconsciousness; and all who derive from east of that line will be basically Norse.

Concerning the Conglomerate this may be said, that admission to one or another of its aspects is obtained by initiation, and that its varied influences prevail wherever its varied rites have been worked long enough, and on a sufficiently high level, to have struck their roots in the earth and built up an enduring subtle form. The Conglomerate is derived from the various Traditions that flourished among the lands washed by the Mediterranean Sea, for European culture is primarily a Mediterranean Tradition, and many prefer to use that term because of the associations implied by the other – associations which have no relation to its use in the Mystery terminology, but which nevertheless influence men's minds.

In the Mediterranean Culture are included the classical influences of Greece and Rome; the Romance influences; the Egyptian influences; the Jewish and Qabalistic influences, and the Christian influences. All of these are so deeply rooted in the Group Soul of these islands that they rank with the native Norse and Keltic cultures in their influence on men's minds. All these, being fused together by the flux of history, constitute a Tradition of incomparable richness and diversity, permitting a wide variety of adaptions to varying conditions.

Over this diversity within unity preside a group of Masters whose task it is to direct the Mysteries in the British Isles with the exception of Southern Ireland, which after long centuries of inclusion in and contribution to the British Tradition, has elected to contract out and be separate. That is the concern of none save the Southern Irish and calls for no comment. Of these Masters, some are of one type, and some of another, but all are brethren, and between them they direct the spiritual destinies of the people of these islands, one of their number, representative of the predominant interest, being the Master of Masters among them.

Their methods of working differ in kind but are directed to the same end – the uniting of the personality with the individuality. The differences lie in the point where the process is started and the point where the stress is laid. The final goal is unity; but as there are many different starting places, so must there be many different routes; some of these converge as they advance, and some do not meet until the final goal.

It will be observed that in all this there is no mention of the Eastern Tradition; that is because there is no place for the Eastern Tradition in the West in the practical workings, though its intellectual and philosophical influence is not be ignored and should, indeed, be cultivated with much benefit. From the foregoing explanations it should be clearly seen why a method that depends for its working on the Eastern Group soul and Place Aura cannot operate in the Western hemisphere. In addition to which there are two important factors to be taken into consideration – the Eastern Culture, or Group Mind, is very much older than the Western; those who achieved maturity of soul and initiation under that culture are ripe for withdrawal from the earth sphere altogether; consequently their attitude towards manifestation differs fundamentally from that of those who are undergoing evolution under the Jurisdiction of the Western Tradition and who are, for the most part, of a much later evolution and in no wise as yet ready to lay aside the discipline of matter. The task of the East is the liberation of the soul from the bonds of matter by the power of the spirit; the task of the West is the conquest of matter by the power of the mind. The liberation of the soul that has achieved this conquest comes later, and the East collectively reached it many centuries ago; yet, when the West collectively arrives at the same place in evolution, it will be upon a higher arc than that wherein the East passed through it because evolution has advanced meanwhile.

Because the two cultures are facing different ways, the younger culture facing downwards into matter and the elder facing upwards into spirit, their destinies, their duties and their methods are entirely different; and as souls are born into one or another according to their age and needs, the methods of the one are not to be exchanged for those of the other lightly or inadvisedly. Nevertheless, each can learn from the other intellectually; but the methods of the one have to undergo profound modification before they can be adapted to the needs of the other. The interchange of cultures has produced a considerable degree of the merging and modification outlook, especially in the East, which is being steadily Westernised; but although the outlook of the West has undergone some modification by eastern influences, and could with profit undergo more, being reminded of things forgotten in this materialistic age, nevertheless it will not be Easternised in the way that the East is becoming Westernised because the future of evolution lies in the West and not in the East. To the East belongs the glory of a great past from which we may learn, but to which we may not return.

The distinction is particularly marked in the difference in the attitude towards the things of the body in the East and West, though this has been modified by the fact that Christianity is an Eastern religion in its origin, even if profoundly modified in its practice. The esoteric attitude of the Western Tradition in such matters is more truly represented by the Greek outlook than by the Christian, and is therefore in some degree at a divergence with the orthodoxy of these islands. It will be noted that the Greeks in their heyday developed the finest flower of human culture that has ever been known, and that it was Greek thought that re-illuminated the Western culture when it had fallen into the darkness of the Middle Ages. The Mystery Tradition is older than any religion that is practised by western man at the present day; all the faiths and modifications of the faiths which he has held, down through the ages, have contributed to its making, each in is turn has served as a plinth for its successor. So will it always be with mankind, whose life is evolving, not static. At each change of Age a great change of culture sets in, and we are in the early stages of such a change. Things will not be again as they were; a new day is dawning and workers are needed to build anew, not to rebuild on the old foundations. For this work, as always, a degree of the Mysteries is thrown open to the light of common day, ceasing to be esoteric, and becoming exoteric. It is for this task that workers are needed. They must be initiates, based in the Mysteries but operating in the outer world.

They work under the Jurisdiction of the Masters of the Western Tradition ruling these islands. Because of the conglomerate nature of the Tradition, and because of certain special work to be done at the present time, it is not only permissible but desirable that colour distinctions should not be drawn. All who are worthy to fight for an empire are worthy of its citizenship. It will be found in practice, however, that there are certain affinities and antipathies among Group Souls, and that the Mongolian and the African have at the present time more affinity with the Western tradition than certain other alien types. Therefore being in sympathy, they can co-operate; whereas those types whose Group Souls hold divergent ideals dominate and change, or to disrupt and weaken. Neither of these things is desirable. Each race has its own destiny to pursue under its own leaders, and change can only come from within, if change be needed.

But in any case, in these Western islands it is the Western Jurisdiction that prevails. Those of other jurisdictions enter here as guests, and a wise man does not try to play host in the house of another.

> *May 1944 – Monte Cassino finally falls to the Allies. The approval is given for Operation Overlord – the Allied invasion of France. D-Day is 6 June 1944 – 150,000 Allied troops pour into Normandy to begin the liberation of Europe.*

Dion Fortune began her esoteric development as a psychologist and over the years maintained this interest. In this letter we see perhaps her last word on the subject. She had developed a considerable sympathy to the approach of Jungian psychology and the little book she recommends by Dr Jolan Jacobi was used as a text book on the Fraternity's introductory study course for a number of years. Although she was well aware of some major differences between the approach of the occultist and psychologist she maintained that each discipline could still contribute much to the other.

MONTHLY LETTER 18 & 19
for May & June 1944

AN INTRODUCTION TO ESOTERIC PSYCHOLOGY

I made the acquaintance of psychology in 1914 when Freud's ideas were first attracting popular attention in this country, and the opinion I then expressed, immature though it was, I have lived to see confirmed – it was not in Freud that psychology would find its Darwin. Though I realised their partial truth, my common sense rejected the Freudian concepts as an incomplete statement of the nature of the soul of man, only applicable to certain types of cases, and the same may be said for Adler's viewpoint. It was not until I came to the study of the Zurich School that I found psychology which could be correlated with esoteric psychology.

The works of Jung cover a very wide range of knowledge and thought; and though this constitutes their chief value for the thinker, it places difficulties in the way of the beginner. I myself am greatly in the debt of Dr Jolan Jacobi, whose very useful book, *The Psychology of C.G. Jung* provides the ground-plan so necessary for the understanding of the wide ranging thought of the man in whom I am satisfied psychology has found its Darwin; whose mind has penetrated to the real nature of man and revealed its workings.

Dr Jung approaches his subject from the empirical aspect of inductive science. He observes phenomena and draws conclusions. But there is another aspect from which the approach can be made – that of the subjective experience of the psychics and mystics of all ages and races; a body of experience that has been continually depositing a crystalline sediment in the form of the Mystery Tradition.

This tradition is just as empirical in its way as the Jungian psychology. It too is based on observation, but the observation of subjective states by the person experiencing them, and the system of thought built up therefrom is not an inductive science but a deductive philosophy.

Both systems have developed their techniques; the one as the applied science of psychotherapy, and the other the art of magic, using that term in its true sense as the method of inducing certain states of consciousness by the use of symbols, thus introducing a connecting link between the two kinds of reality, the subjective and the objective, instead of relying on their accidental impact as in the case of spontaneous as distinguished from induced experience of extended consciousness.

Psychology has developed a very fine and sensitive technique for exploring the surface of the mind, and has begun to venture out into the hinterland which lies behind the coastal plain of consciousness that is washed by the great ocean of objective experience. It has acquired great experience in the best methods of jungle warfare in those overgrown regions of lush phantasy. But of the geography of the mountain ranges that lie behind the coastal belt, whose summits rise clear of the mists of the lower levels into the high rare air of eternity and through whose gorges wind passes that lead to the central plateau where the spirit dwells apart – of all that rich realm of the hinterland and their Interior Castles, psychology knows only what it can deduce from the exoteric aspect of myths to whose esoteric meaning it lacks the keys.

For its technique it depends on the utilisation of the material spontaneously produced by dreams; an excellent means of exploring the personal unconscious that lies near the surface, but by no means so effective for entering the innermost as the methods developed by mystics down through the ages of human experience and crystallised in Mystery Tradition and ritual initiation.

The more one sees of the Jungian method of psycho-analysis, the more clearly does one realise what good use the ancients made of their intuitive technique. Their thought seems alien and superstitious to moderns because it is not according to their convention, a convention that recognises only one kind of thinking, a thinking carried on in words. But there is another kind of thinking which is an equally efficacious instrument for arriving at the truth. This thinking is carried on in pictorial images instead of word images; and the images are combined together into pictures instead of sentences; but the pictures have their own grammar and logic in their own idiom, and for dealing with certain kinds of material they are far superior to the verbal method, though translation into the modern idiom is the final stage of the process.

In both psychology and magic the true art lies in the reduction of the material made available to consciousness, whether derived from the spontaneous dream or induced vision, to such form that it is readily assimilable by the understanding and related to the science and art of living. For this purpose psychology has in dream analysis through free association a technique for gaining access to the deeper levels of consciousness, and in particular for picking out a given factor at will and working with it and no other, which is unknown to psychology – so far, at any rate, as the published word reveals it.

There may be psychologists who are occultists, but as far as my experience goes, there are precious few occultists who are psychologists, and those that are keep their knowledge in watertight compartments for the good and excellent reason that they fear that if they did not, they would destroy the foundations on which they stand. This would be true in the case of the Freudian psychology which is a reductive psychology, reducing the building to the bricks, and then tipping a barrow-load of rubble out on the lecture platform and crying "Behold the stuff of which the vision of the architect is made!"

The Jungian psychology takes account of the fact that the architect builds with bricks, girders and other unpicturesque raw material; but it also takes account of the fact that edifices are not run up aimlessly. There is purpose in their building; they serve human needs and activities. The Jungian analyst uses the methods of the archaeologist, not the demolition gang. He tries to reconstruct from the stratified fragments the kind of life that was lived when Troy was an inhabited city. It is a more interesting, more fruitful, and incidentally a much cleaner occupation than the Freudian method.

With Jungian psychology the ancient Mystery Tradition can join hands. They may not speak the same language, but they have the same outlook. All that is needed is a Rosetta Stone bearing parallel inscriptions in different languages, the known and the unknown, to enable translation to begin and an immense wealth of data and experience to be made available for both sides of the council table.

Psychologists have long been at work trying to penetrate the mystery symbolism from the hither side of the Veil of the Temple. Unfortunately they made use of the Freudian reductive technique of "nothing but", and the Temple of the Mysteries soon lay in a heap of rubble at their feet, its beauty destroyed and its significance lost. They were then able to explore at their leisure the drains and cess-pools under the foundations and discover to their delight that the soul, like the body, has certain needs that require sanitary arrangements; but is such a discovery, absorbing though it may be to those who have a taste for such things, any adequate substitute for the domes and spires of the architect's vision? Nor was the secret of the purpose of such a building to be deduced from its footings even by the most careful comparison with similar structures extant today. A railway station and a cathedral are not so dissimilar in their ground plans that a person ignorant of the nature of both might not confuse them in an age that has only had experience of aerodromes. Men's needs do not alter down through the ages, but only his methods of serving them.

Let us, for a change, approach psychology from the yonder side of the Veil of the Mysteries. It will be an exercise not without its practical value, in my humble opinion. I would say to my fellow occultists, who love me not because of the amount of debunking I have done in my time: Here is something by which you can check up on your findings and learn what is true and what is not, if you have a liking for such a proceeding. To the psychologists I would say: Here is no poor relation, no illegitimate child of orthodoxy, but an heir to great estates, born of ancient lineage, coming with both hands full of jewels.

For the understanding of what I have to say it will be necessary to have a working knowledge of both occultism and psychology, for I do not pretend to begin at the beginning and lay the foundations of knowledge of either science in the minds of my readers. The minimum necessary can, however, be acquired from the study of two books, that by Dr Jacobi to which I have already referred, and my own *Mystical Qabalah*.

The long article that appeared in Monthly Letters 18 and 19 is a somewhat technical one, and gives some idea of what the Fraternity expected of its initiates. Geburah, as Qabalistic students will know, is one of the spheres of the Qabalistic Tree of Life that represents God in the aspect of Severity, and within its symbolism are to be found images such as sword, spear, scourge and chain. In terms of esoteric grades it relates to that of Adeptus Major, of whom, it should be said, there are not many around, although there is no lack of examples of the unbalanced expression of this divine principle in humanity at large. It is not unfitting that such a series of meditations should be appropriate towards the end of a world encompassing war, the aftermath of which was to reveal unspeakable atrocities and the need for some sort of court of international justice to handle such crimes against humanity. Regrettably, the course of events over the ensuing seventy years has hardly made these concerns a thing of the past.

Although not specifically stated, the tone of this material is as from one of the Inner Plane Adepti rather than from Dion Fortune herself, although there is of course an intermediate zone whereby the skilled initiate mediator becomes 'impressed' or 'inspired' rather than 'ensouled' or 'entranced' for the purpose of communication.

CONCERNING THE USE OF THE SWORD OF GEBURAH

I.

The initiation of the Sphere of Geburah is that of Adeptus Major. Only one of the Greater Adepts can use the Power of the Sword, and unless he can use it, he is not a Greater Adept. The world cannot be ruled by love alone, but only by power in equilibrium, justice and mercy kissing each other.

The four symbols of Geburah are the Sword, the cutting instrument which severs and cuts off; the Spear, the piercing instrument which is a projection and extension of force, a solid ray as it were, emanating on the plane of Malkuth; the Scourge, the punishing instrument that stings but does not slay and whose use is to stimulate to redemption; the Chain is the restraining instrument which imposes limits on wilful evil. These four sacred symbols are the weapons of Geburah, and the Greater Adept must be expert in their use.

The tasks of Geburah, dual tasks, as all must be that deal in the sphere of manifestation, are to stimulate and to withstand, these being the positive and negative aspects of the work of a Greater Adept. At a certain stage upon the Path, initiates pass out of the mild sphere of Tiphareth and enter that of the severity of Justice. The Adept who initiates here must know no mercy, for cosmic law knows none, and what he spares, the Lords of Destiny, who rule over evolution, will punish. He aspires high who submits himself to the tests of Major Adepthood, and he must abide his fate. Here is no place for folly or weakness. Good intentions avail him nothing in the sphere of Justice, nor may ignorance be pleaded in extenuation. Achievement is the only test and all weakness is burnt away.

It is not the greatness of the strength that constitutes the test of this Sphere, but its perfection in proportion. An ant is stronger than a man in proportion to its size, yet Nature does not demand of an ant that it shall be as strong as a man, but only that it shall have the due strength of an ant. So of a simple nature we do not demand that it shall be as strong as a world leader, but only that it shall have the element of strength proportionate to its gifts; for lack of courage can invalidate the powers of the most gifted creatures, making them of no avail.

The initiate of Geburah submits himself to the tests of Geburah, which try his courage and endurance; and if he be not found wanting in these, the Sword of Justice is placed in his hand and he becomes a Greater Adept. He must then wield the Sword with wisdom and courage, for as the Yetziratic Text has it, courage is the characteristic virtue of Geburah, which emanates from the primordial depths of Chokmah, Wisdom.

Mercy is not in this Sphere, yet emanates it; and this is a paradox in which is to be found deep meaning. The wielder of the Sword of Geburah knows no mercy, but continues to the end. But even as Geburah was emanated from Gedulah, Mercy, when the Lightning Flash descends down the Tree, so in its turn it emanates Beauty in the centre of the Pillar of Equilibrium, which, "causes the influence to flow into all the reservoirs of blessing and wherein is seen the Vision of the Harmony of Things and wherein are performed the Mysteries of the Crucifixion."

Remember that it is said in the Mysteries that no degree becomes functional till the next degree has been conferred, so mighty works of redemption in Tiphareth do not begin until the Initiation of Geburah has been undergone. Thus is Geburah balanced in equilibrium between Mercy and Beauty, and this is the secret of its work.

In the great stories of the Table Round which are the Glyphs of Geburah, even as the legend of the Graal is the Glyph of Tiphareth, the Knights of King Arthur are famed for their strength towards the strong, their mercy to the weak, and their personal beauty. Thus does Geburah confer the knighthood of the Mysteries. The army is terrible with beautiful banners. Beauty is the true mean, and resides in right proportion. So always must the power of Geburah be wielded in right proportion and in wisdom.

The Adept of Geburah may not deal in Mercy. When he has performed his work, initiation passes out of his hands into the Sphere of Mercy; but in his hands, Mercy would be but weakness, which in folly suffers evil to multiply or yields to the temptations of sloth. Ruthless and calm he abides, the servant of cosmic law, and Mercy and Beauty are the fruit of his works.

Whoso serves in the Sphere of Geburah as an Adeptus Major lays his soul upon the Altar of Sacrifice. When he invokes justice upon another, he appears with him before the Bar of Divine Justice and is judged equally with him. Therefore must his hands be clean and his heart free from guile; for guile and Geburah do not abide together, the one counteracting the other. Immediately below Geburah, in Hod, Mercury, is the Sphere of Guile, even as immediately above this most dynamic of the Sephiroth is the Sphere of Saturn, the giver of stability. Whoso has strength needs no guile, though guile be used to cause evil to destroy itself; but this is not the work of Geburah, and when the sword is invoked the fight must be straightforward.

Whoso takes in hand the sword must abide its judgement. If he err, he will perish by the sword. He may not wield it save in the name of Justice; yet he may wield it to ensure justice for himself as well as for others, for is he not also one of God's children? Dare to invoke the might of Geburah if your heart be pure and your hands clean. Whosoever has not known the experience of the Initiation of the Sword cannot pass on to the higher Degrees, for it is by the power of the brave that evil is withstood. By the

Sword evil is cut off from its source of power; by the thrust of the Spear its onslaught is checked; by the Scourge are its exponents schooled, and by the Chain are they restrained.

The two greater implements of Geburah work in the sphere of abstract force, and the two lesser in the sphere of its manifestation through personalities. Never forget, in wielding the powers of Geburah, that the most effectual defence is attack. Therefore do not be afraid to drive at evil with the thrust of the Spear, nor think it incumbent upon you to await its onslaught passively. But remember that in all things there is a rhythm, and even the most dynamic of spheres alternates between activity and passivity; but until the thrust of the Spear has been given, the work has not begun. Passivity is folly in Geburah. There is a method whereby evil is turned back upon itself and caused to sting itself to death with its own venom, but this is not the method of Geburah; it belongs to Hod, which lies immediately beneath the Fiery Sphere upon the Pillar of Severity; and there is a method of working whereby the interplay of the Sephiroth, equilibrating among themselves, is used, and Mars can pass on to Mercury, and Mercury back to Mars, the task of salvation by destruction.

II.

The Sephirah Hod is the Basal Station of the Pillar of Severity, even as Binah is its Apical Station. No Sephirah can ever be considered by itself, for it stands in terms of relationship, evolutional and functional, to other Sephiroth according to circumstances. In considering problems arising in the Sphere of Severity, the Pillar of Severity as a whole must be taken into account. The function of the Sephirah Binah is, however, of so abstract and universal a nature that it does not require separate consideration when practical applications are under discussion. It represents forces of stability and inertia and is the basis of all organisation. It reflects into Chesed and back into Hod; whereas Chokmah, the dynamic factor, reflects into Geburah and back into Netzach, thus imparting to the central Sephirah of the Pillar of Severity its dynamic aspect.

Hod is a many-sided Sephirah, as is indicated by the symbolic form of an Hermaphrodite attributed to it. It is associated with Hermes, who lent his sandals and shield to Perseus for the slaying of the Gorgon in the name of Justice, by which myth we may discern the nature of its connection with Geburah. The winged sandals lent the swiftness of thought to the feet of the hero, and in the polished shield he saw reflected as in a mirror the deadly head of the Gorgon, thus sustaining no harm from her glances.

Considered from the standpoint of the works of justice, we see in Mars the Lord of Tactics and in Mercury the Master of Strategy. Hod or Mercury likewise represents the human mind; for evolution has advanced up the Tree through its sphere, thus causing it to become organised in terms of consciousness. It is therefore no formless sphere of force, as is Geburah, but a sphere wherein mind operates in terms of that consciousness developed in Malkuth.

When the powers of Geburah descend into Malkuth, they reflect through Hod, wherein they undergo transmutation. Thus it is that with the advance of evolution brute force prevails less and less and the powers of the mind count for more. But let it never be forgotten that Mercury is a god of dual nature, and that in his evil aspect he is the Lord of Lies. Beware of this side of his nature when invoking him, and let the chivalry of the forthright Geburah guard you against it, even as the shrewd skill of Mercury directs the blind force of the sword.

In the sphere of Hermes that relates to Geburah it is well to rely upon the methods of Perseus, and let the sandals of swiftness keep you out of harm's way by virtue of the penetrative power of thought which discerns the direction of the attack and evades it. Likewise use the shield of Hermes to gaze in as into a mirror, and do not use it as a weapon with which to strike the adversary. Hod is the sphere of mind, and there are certain factors in mind that make it a two-edged weapon when used for attack. It is too closely connected with the soul for such usage. It should be your aim, when using the powers of Hod in the work of Geburah, to cause your adversary to destroy himself with his own venom rather than to destroy him with your own hand. In this way you avoid the reaction that falls upon those who take up the sword if the forces be not balanced exactly; and who, in the heat of battle, can hope so to balance them?

When wielding the sword of Geburah, gaze into the shield of Hermes and not upon the face of the Adversary. Set the forces of Geburah in motion with sword or spear, then flit aside on the winged sandals of wisdom and let the rhythm change over from sword to shield. The cosmic forces will not work for you unless you set them in motion; but having set them in motion, stand aside and let them fight for you. Then, when they have done their work, advance again, and discipline with the scourge or restrain with the chain as need shall arise. Remember always that after the work of the sword, the scourge or chain is needed to restrain the reaction, and you cannot rest immediately upon your laurels. These things concern the dark Pillar of Severity, which ever works in polarity with the bright Pillar of Mercy, thus establishing equilibrium.

It has been said that those who take the sword shall perish by the sword, and that you resist not evil. It must ever be borne in mind when considering such sayings, and many others, that the grade of the hearer must be taken into consideration. As another saying has it, there is milk for babes and strong meat for strong men. Geburah is a grade, and a high grade, in the Hierarchy of the Mysteries. Upon its initiates devolves a very serious responsibility. The powers of the Macrocosm can only function in the world of men through the medium of men's souls. No special miracle will smite from heaven the enemies of God, but men may arise, dedicated and courageous men; men of might and vision, and through them the cosmic powers work. To them is opportunity given; around them the powers are organised, and through them justice is done and the way cleared for the Lords of Light. In meeting aggression with mildness, do not forget that time plays a part in the suffering of the victims of the oppressor, and there is a limit to the time that they can endure, and why should you show mercy to the evil at the cost of the sufferings of the innocent?

There is another saying which says: Smite, and spare not. Cruelty and oppression can never learn the evil of their ways in any school save that of suffering. If you say to the oppressor, Cease to do evil and learn to do good, and it shall be well with you, he will answer, It is well with me now. If, having conquered him with the sword and the spear, you let him be the one to cry peace, when it serves his purpose he will again take up the weapons of aggression, knowing that when it serves his purpose he can cry peace once more. He has much to gain and little to lose by his acts of aggression, if, when he has had enough of strife he can count on mercy. But if he knows that the scourge and the chain wait to complete the work begun by the sword and the spear, he will count the cost before he embarks upon his evil ways afresh, and the innocent and the simple shall sleep safe and reap where they have sown.

Until the final day, the men of Geburah, its initiates, and servants, must keep guard over the peace of the world to defend the defenceless and do justice among men, restraining the strong and upholding the weak. There is no other way whereby God's will may be made to prevail, and it is folly to think otherwise. Mercy has its place, but only as the equilibrator of Justice. And Justice has its place, but as the equilibrator of Mercy.

The equilibrium induced by the counteracting influences of the Pairs of Opposites is for ever the Law of Manifestation. The watch must be kept in the world of men and in the Unseen World of Causation; the servants of justice may not rest from their arms, but must be ever at their posts lest the defenceless fall victims to the oppressor. It is the task of the strong to guard the weak and ensure them justice. They may not refuse battle without dishonour. When there is strife, they must wield arms upon one side or the other.

Those who tread the Path pass on from grade to grade. Not all are in the grade of Geburah, but none may evade the grade and gain the goal. And remember this – to fail a grade does not mean merely that you go back to the grade below, but that you return to the commencement of the Path and start all over again. It may be that by virtue of the experience gained thereon you shall pass onwards swiftly, but it does mean, it cannot mean other, than that those who cannot or dare not or will not wield the sword of Geburah when duty calls must return to the hewing of wood and the drawing of water for a while.

Likewise, even as there is a Tree in every Sephirah, so there is a sphere of Geburah in the soul of every man. In the soul of the balanced being – and none other can achieve – all the Sephiroth are of equal power, each after its kind. Thus, and thus only can equilibrium be achieved. According to its stage of evolution will be the degree of conscious activation of the Sephiroth in the Microcosm, and according to the path by which the soul has come will be the proportional development among them. This may be gravely irregular if development has been ill-balanced, as it is liable to be if superstition and not wisdom direct the choice or rejection of experience. Beyond the level of individualisation, the Sephiroth function in accordance with the activities of the corresponding macrocosmic spheres as mediating to them through the group soul of the race to which they belong. Here again, force may be well or ill-balanced according to the wisdom and justice that rule the racial tradition. Do not expect perfection in the sphere of manifestation, for when perfection is reached, the universe enters upon the Night of the Gods and sinks into its rest in the Unmanifest. As long as life endures the discipline of manifestation, the Servers of Geburah must stand on guard to see to it that unbalanced force is kept within due bounds.

There is a grade of initiation wherein the initiate must enter the sphere of Geburah and abide therein to learn its lessons, and the less of Geburah there is in him, the longer must he abide there. He who is already a man of the sword passes on swiftly. There are times of crisis and emergency when even those who have passed on to the Sphere of Mercy may be recalled to man the ramparts of Geburah, and none may refuse the call, for who are they to keep their garments unspotted from the world? The stains of toil and the scars of battle are more honourable insignia than the spotless robe of negation. Who was the cleaner at the end of the Day of Crucifixion, Herod or his Victim? No greater love is possible than to give one's life in selfless service, and such service comprises more than the binding up of the wounds made by aggression, waiting till the victim is injured before aiding him. It means also to seek out aggression in its stronghold and overthrow it so that it may have no victims. The work of succour is good, but the work of prevention is better, and the aggressor can only be convinced of the error of his ways by making them unprofitable and painful. The only appeal that touches the heart of a ruthless and cruel man is that of pain to his own person. The way to his heart is through his skin.

Distinguish, however, between the strong man who is ruthless in the selfish use of his strength and the weak and unprincipled man who plays jackal to the tiger. For such it is enough to make evil unprofitable for them to cease from it, but they can never be trusted not to return to their vomit if it suits them; therefore, although it is not necessary to apply the scourge to their skin, as in the case of the strong who have chosen evil, it is advisable to keep it hanging within their sight and to crack it occasionally as an encouragement to persevere in the laborious paths of virtue, for not otherwise can virtue be sustained that is not strong enough to sustain itself.

In judging men, and in meting out punishment and mercy, remember that on the plane of manifestation it is the personality alone that is dealt with; you must deal with them as they are in this incarnation, though taking account of what they were in past incarnations which makes them what they are now, and taking account also of the racial destiny in which they are involved. For in reincarnating the soul abides by the line of tradition, returning where it belongs by nature and custom, save in the case of those who are freed from their bondage in the group soul by virtue of their development.

By teaching the lesson to individuals is the soul of a race instructed. Individuals, in the mass, can drag a race in the dust; individuals, in the mass, can raise it to great heights. This they can do apart from leadership if the spirit of the race is stirring. No leader can lead unless the led follow. It is the spirit of the race that brings forth the leaders; those who speak with another breath are voices crying in the wilderness where there are none to heed. The spirit of the race can bring forth and bring to power nobility, wisdom, courage, and sound minds among its leaders; it can also bring forth demons in human form. It happens sometimes, however, though these times grow rarer as more and more among men become individualised and freed from their bondage to the group soul, that one man may gain dominion over a race and direct its course. This can never be other than evil, for power corrupts. Where there is a great gulf fixed between the leaders and the led you may know that this evil has occurred and that it forebodes disaster. When the spirit of the race itself has given birth to the leaders that guide its destiny, the hierarchy is pyramidal, and the ranks of leadership are constantly recruited from the masses.

If the scene is witnessed of a royal court of great splendour while darkness is upon the face of the land, know that here is a dynasty that will not endure but the people are innocent of evil. If the scene be that of widespread and intelligent co-operation with the workers of oppression, know that the soul of the people is involved, and must share in the expiation. In such a land, only the strong and the ruthless are safe, and only they survive. Each child must be reared in the tenets of ruthlessness and strength if he in his turn is to survive. Goodness and gentleness and justice are without hope and power. Yet even in such a land they are absent from the human heart, for such is the nature of man, who is good as well as evil and evil as well as good, so that there is always hope for him, though there is always danger from him. Make such a land safe for goodness and mercy and they will raise their heads and flourish, but how can they prevail against the forces of organised evil? You will not dispose of evil by making terms with his servants. Destroy the channels of evil; open the channels of good, and good will multiply as the corn stifles the well-hoed weeds. What shall it avail to break a nation that has gone over to evil and leave it broken for evil to re-organise? Nor is it even enough to destroy the organisation of evil; good must be organised in its place. The clearest distinction between evil and good is to be found in the spirit of separateness and unity that prevails. Evil always leans to separateness and good to unity. When good builds an empire it holds it by integrating it, thus bringing the blessings of civilisation to backward races. When evil builds it, it is founded upon the subjugation and exploitation of the conquered peoples. Those who dwell in glass houses must not throw stones. Look well to the ways of your own empire as well as to the imperial ambitions of others.

The power of good gains strength by integration. Draw into the building of the New Age all men of goodwill wherever they may be found. Undermine the powers of organised evil by integrating the forces of good within its sphere and uniting them with the common weal of the world's life. Provide a channel of expression for forces that have been directed into evil ways but are not in themselves evil. Deny the dignity of citizenship to none who as individuals may prove themselves worthy. Remember that it is not in the power of the weak to resist their environment, and that weakness is a misfortune, not a crime. Let Geburah deal with the strong, but let Gedulah guide the weak.

It seems fitting that we close this volume, not with a Weekly or Monthly Letter, but with the Trance Address given to the assembled Fraternity on the occasion of the Vernal Equinox of 1944. The European war would be won in a little over a year's time, and the communicator is plainly confident of this fact as he reviews the working of the group as it prepares itself for the post-war era.

An interesting element in this talk is the concept of a Divine Aspect known as the Destroyer. In one sense this relates to the material on Geburah previously communicated, although in more general terms it is the winter aspect of the four-fold cycle of nature, but applied to the rise and fall of civilisations and nations. It is appropriate to a time when much that was of the old order would pass away, to make way for the new.

Little was it realised either, it would seem, that this would include Dion Fortune too, who was to pass away in the January of 1946. Yet there are in this script prophetic words of comfort: "Surrender yourself to the Destroyer when he calls you in the sure and certain hope of a glorious resurrection; death is the gate of new life even as is birth, and no more to be feared or deplored ..."

TRANCE ADDRESS GIVEN AT THE VERNAL EQUINOX 25th March 1944

Greetings, my Brethren –
We are met together at this the Vernal Equinox of one thousand nine hundred and forty-four. This date marks an end and a beginning. Your Lodge working, which it is my duty and happiness to inspect, reflects that end and that beginning. You have achieved a ritual working of great excellence. Within the simplicity of your ceremony has been built up power and beauty in equilibrium – I especially noted the beauty of the voices. Such polished working, without a jarring note, is necessary for the manifestation of power in full splendour. The working is satisfactory, set it as your standard; it represents achievement, and I congratulate you.

I speak to you first of the conditions in which you find yourselves, individually as men and women of your race, and collectively as a Brotherhood. You find yourselves in the darkness of the dawn with the rim of the rising sun just appearing above the Eastern horizon. For your information it is necessary that you should be informed of the proximate developments; note this, affairs move fast now, the tides of affairs on the Inner Planes are now flowing. In your mundane working and organisation you can do anything for which you have the conditions and the workers; proceed therefore according to your judgement and opportunity. What you build now will stand; do not, however, go forth into the outer world, but remain within the Temple behind closed doors; conditions in the outer world are not yet ready, but within the Temple conditions are ready, and you can go forward in the name of the Mysteries. I thank those who have remained faithful through the long hours of darkness and slack water, under great difficulties, and in many cases in great danger. It is harder thus to keep the night watch than to advance with the dawn. There is a blessing of an especial nature on those who have kept the night watch.

We now advance to the dawn of a new epoch, old things are passing away, all things are becoming new; Our Lord said, "I have yet many things to tell you but you cannot bear them now." I say I have many things to tell you and you can bear them now. It is not easy working for you because all grades are reduced to a single grade, consequently into that single grade must come workings that rightly belong to the higher grades, and those who are of that grade must do as best they can. They have thus great privileges but also great difficulties; it is not easy for them but I bid them be of good cheer. If they have it in them to advance to the higher grades whose impact they must thus bear untrained and unprepared they will achieve. Even though the path be somewhat rough to their feet – for those who come after it will be easier by virtue of the sacrifices and the endurance of those who achieved under difficulties.

I wish today to give you certain teaching that you may better understand the work that is being done and the problems you are called upon to solve in the course of it. Some of you have heard all this before, but some of you hear it for the first time; all of you can profit by considering it. For it may be that you have made progress since last you heard it and will now perceive in the teaching what you could not see before.

All begins in unity and ends in unity – there is one God. The exoteric Church knows the Godhead as a Trinity, the esoteric Temple knows the Godhead as a quaternary. Consider the moon; you gaze upon her face, and she always presents the same face to you. Consider her silvery disc as divided into four segments; you see the whole of one, and the half of two, and one you never see at all. But you know it must be there for no front can exist without a back; so, brightly as shines the moon, she needs must have a dark side. So it is with the Godhead; you see the whole of one segment (that aspect of the Godhead which relates to the epoch), you see the latter half of the preceding aspect and the first half of the succeeding aspect and there is a dark side which you do not see, though you know it must be there if you are an initiate.

Of the Trinitarian aspect we know God the Primordial Father of which segment we see the latter half, the earlier having passed away from human sight with the passage of cosmic time. We see the whole of that segment which constitutes the second person of the Trinity, God the Son, God made manifest in human form. We see the first half of that segment which represents the third person of the Trinity, God the Holy Spirit; the second half of that segment has not yet manifested on earth, and can only be known to those who can rise to a level of consciousness beyond brain-consciousness.

The fourth side is an aspect of the Godhead known only to initiates, and herein is a deep truth which you must know if you would serve in the Temple. The first person of the Quaternary is God the Creator, the Giver of Life; the second is God the Redeemer, the Preserver of Life; the Third is God the Illuminator, the Renewer of Life; the fourth is God the Destroyer, the Taker of Life. All these are aspects of the one God, the Destroyer no less than the Redeemer, for the Destroyer makes all things new and opens the doors to the incoming Light made manifest through God the Creator. Fear not the Destroyer; He is true God, and His servants are great initiates. That is the secret of the Temple without which cannot work the Mystery Rituals.

Surrender yourself to the Destroyer when he calls you in the sure and certain hope of a glorious resurrection; death is the gate of new life even as is birth and no more to be feared or deplored: and premature death is as regrettable as premature birth. Those who die through their own error die prematurely, no other death is premature – even in youth. Those who die in childhood do not die prematurely; of necessity there are souls that come into incarnation for certain purposes in order that they may die properly. There are those whose previous death has been attended by some difficulty or pathology; they are born in order to die properly. There are those now (and they are many) who are dying in the flower of their youth, their manhood unenjoyed and unfulfilled, and they are of our best; but they are not dying prematurely, they are being sent for from the Inner Planes that they may build a new era. For that purpose they were born in the throes of the last world war; many of them died in that war and reincarnated as volunteers to die again in this in order that the New Age may be born through them. Such are known by their intuitive knowledge of the work to be done and their vision of things to come. They are called over to fulfil the chosen purpose; and no man goes who is not a volunteer. They retain the Personalities of the incarnation in which they were born and died, in contradistinction to those who go over, their destiny fulfilled, their lessons learned, who absorb the essences of their Personality and cast off the empty shell to disintegrate. These, the pioneers of the New Age, retain their Personalities, as do the Masters whom they serve, in order that they may work in the earth's atmosphere. These it is who are bringing in the New Age; those who die the sacrificial death die with power.

Those on the mundane plane who are dedicated also die; they die to self, they die to separateness; they too rise to the glorious resurrection of the initiate illuminated. Those on the mundane plane, those on the Inner Planes, all dead, work together – all dead to the world, all rising together in a glorious resurrection of illumination, all playing their part in the Great Work – to wit, the Redemption of man.

The epochs of the world in the slow moving of evolutionary time pass through the phases of the four aspects of the Godhead as if the moon revolved upon its axis. The age of God the Giver of Life belongs to the past, the age of God the Holy Spirit is dawning. But each soul goes through these phases in its progress from death to birth, during which all that is vile and unpleasant in it is disintegrating.

The immature soul is under the jurisdiction of God the Giver of Life; the fully developed soul passes over to the jurisdiction of God the Redeemer; the more highly evolved soul passes on to God the Illuminator; the dying soul passes on to God the Destroyer Who maketh all things new and brings rebirth on a higher arc, all errors being corrected.

Each age of man, like each age of the Earth, is under the jurisdiction of an aspect of the Godhead; none may be abrogated and none forestalled. Those who have not known God the Giver of Life made manifest in nature cannot know rightly God the Redeemer made manifest in civilisation, and they who have not known the saving spirit of the Christ draw not nigh the Pentecostal Flames. Those who are not thus ready for illumination sleep throughout in nether death … asleep. Those who are ready go over in full consciousness and are born remembering the splendours of another place.

Each man lives his own life in his own age and his own place. None may live for another, and none should judge for another. Be loyal to your own truth at all costs, for it is your only sound foundation.

The blessing of the Masters is upon all who serve.

MEDITATION SUBJECTS
FOR THE WEEKLY LETTERS

1.   8.10.39   The realisation that a single and indivisible Life ensouls all men. Therefore, although we are obliged to wage war, we must not hate, for hate will only breed fresh wars.

2.   15.10.39   Making contact with the spiritual influences ruling our race, using for this purpose the symbol of the Rose upon the Cross.

3.   22.10.39   The inevitableness of the victory of cosmic law over unbalanced force; therefore there is no need for fear.

4.   29.10.39   A repetition of last week's work which requires further building.

5.   5.11.39   The constructive peace that is to follow the war, based upon unselfishness and co-operation balanced by justice and strength.

6.   12.11.39   The neutralising of unbalanced force by spiritual influences.

7.   19.11.39   The realisation of the Rings and the Rays swinging into being.

8.   26.11.39   To realise the comradeship of the Elder Brethren.

9.   3.12.39   To establish personal contact with a Master in order that we may stabilise our own conditions.

10.   10.12.39   The rhythm and equilibrium of the pairs of opposites as applied to government.

11.   17.12.39   Dedicate yourself to the service of the Masters of Wisdom, and experiment with the Ray Colours to gain experience.

12.   7.1.40   Realisation of the function of the Tide of Destruction in clearing the ground.

13.   14.1.40   To assert the rule of law, absolute and inescapable.

14.   21.1.40   To invoke the purifying Tides of Destruction upon whatever is obsolete, selfish and inefficient in our country.

15.   28.1.40   Meditate on the angelic Presences guarding the land.

16.   4.2.40   Meditate upon the spiritual factors behind the new life impulse.

17.   11.2.40   The formulation of the Triangle.

18.   18.2.40   Meditate on the conjoined symbols.

19.   25.2.40   Meditate on the Rod of Power.

20.   3.3.40   Meditate on the *Abuse* of the Rod of Power.

21.	10.3.40	Meditate on the direction in which the Diamond Sceptre points.
22.	17.3.40	The direction in which Merlin points the Diamond Sceptre.
23.	7.4.40	Meditate on the new Equinoctial Tide.
24.	14.4.40	The Invisible Powers with which we are co-operating.
25.	21.4.40	The Angelic patrol of the coasts of Great Britain, extended, for those who care to undertake the task, as described.
26.	28.4.40	While still maintaining the Angelic Patrol, meditate upon the significance of the Figure in the Purple Ray.
27.	5.5.40	The spiritual influences of the new era that supply the real strength of the war effort.
28.	26.5.40	The irresistible momentum of evolving life, of which the organisation of the Commonwealth of Nations is the next stage.
29.	2.6.40	The spiritual nature of our war aims and the cosmic power that is behind them to bring them to pass.
30.	9.6.40	The three-chambered Mount of Illumination.
31.	16.6.40	The drawing down of spiritual power into the war effort.
32.	23.6.40	Visualise the great bar of diamond light stretching from this country right across France to Africa.
33.	30.6.40	Build up the picture of the Chapel of the Graal and meditate therein.
34.	7.7.40	The counteracting of subversive telepathy by the power of spiritual disciplines.
35.	14.7.40	The Hill of Vision and the Triangle of Power.
36.	4.8.40	Living our own lives under the influence of the new life impulse.
37.	11 .8.40	The Threefold Glyph in relation to the rebuilding of national life after the war.
38.	18.8.40	The spiritual principles of national life.
39.	25.8.40	Nobility in national life.
40.	1.9.40	The rising tide of new life.
41.	8.9.40	The Supreme Sacrifice. (Given under instruction. We are apparently going to receive teaching on the subject of co-operation with the Invisible Helpers.)
42.	15.9.40	The power that can be brought through by the use of our symbols.

43. 22.9.40 The Formulae of the Three Powers.

44. 29.9.40 The Relationship between the Formula of the Cross and the Formula of the Pentagram.

45. 6.10.40 The Power of Silence to bring Serenity.

46. 13.10.40 All existing standards to be placed on the altar, and the fire of Truth invoked upon them.

47. 20.10.40 May the Great Ones of the Holy Rosicrucian Order bless and protect the dedicated priesthood and the dedicated places. (This formula can be used as a mantram or litany, and will be found a powerful protection by those who use it as well as for those for whom it is used.)

48. 27.10.40 The ideals that give rise to the archetypal ideas that shall direct and control the evolutionary forces.

49. 3.11.40 The Formula of the Red Ray.

50. 10.11.40 The Use of the Formula of the Red Ray as an Act of Self Immolation.

51. 24.11.40 The Qualities of the Initiate.

52. 1.12.40 The Invocation of Personal Protection.

53. 8.12.40 Self Preparation on the Lines laid down in this Letter.

54. 15.12.40 Democracy based on the Laws of Evolving Life.

55. 22.12.40 The spirit that must inspire reconstruction.

56. 12.1.41 The Threefold Glyph in relation to Human Life Values.

57. 19.1.41 The Opening of the Mysteries.

58. 26.1.41 The technique and the use of symbolism.

59. 2.2.41 The Relationship of the Individuality and the Personality.

60. 9.2.41 The appeal to the idealism of the mass mind of the race.

61. 16.2.41 The Breaking of the Vicious Circle of Hate and Fear and Need.

62. 23.2.41 The Four Archangels keeping Watch over these Islands.

63. 2.3.41 The laying upon the altar of all we have, and are, and hope for.

64. 9.3.41 The overcoming of the fear of frustration and loss by meditating on the cosmic life.

65. 16.3.41 The attack on the cloud of an astral evil over Germany.

66. 23.3.41 Self-healing through the Christ-force.

67.	30.3.41	There must be a new formulation of religion for the new age.
68.	6.4.41	The Rose Cross in the Hall of Learning.
69.	20.4.41	The importance of the invisible realities to the national effort.
70.	27.4.41	The power of the technique outlined.
71.	4.5.41	The Principle of Unity.
72.	11.5.41	The Unity underlying Diversity.
73.	18.5.41	The use of the symbolic act in mind work.
74.	25.5.41	Contact with Tradition.
75.	1.6.41	Wisdom, Strength, and Proportion in Harmonised Balance.
76.	8.6.41	The level of racial consciousness and national personality.
77.	15.6.41	The Significance of the Threefold Glyph in Relation to the Organisation of the New Age.
78.	22.6.41	Invocation of the men to appear now that the hour has struck.
79.	29.6.41	The Dedicated Personality as a Channel of Spiritual Force.
80.	6.7.41	Invocation for the sending of the leaders of the New Age.
81.	13.7.41	War as a Sacrament.
82.	20.7.41	The Spirit of Social Organisation.
83.	27.7.41	The three functions of woman.
84.	21.9.41	Self-sacrifice, Leadership, Reconstruction.
85.	28.9.41	The Intelligence to Make Sacrifices for the Ideals of the New Age.
86.	5.10.41	Making the Group Mind of the Race aware of the Risk of Telepathic Suggestion. (Note: Protect yourself by invoking the Power of the Christ while doing so.)
87.	12.10.41	The Waking of Arthur.
88.	19.10.41	Sympathy with the Life Urge.
89.	26.10.41	The Cosmic Forces choosing their own Channels.
90.	2.11.41	The Protecting Power of the Forces for which we are building a Channel.
91.	9.11.41	The Mystery Tradition, of which our meditation group forms a part.
92.	16.11.41	The New Order that shall include Germany.

93. 23.11.41 A New Age, not reconstruction.

94. 30.11.41 The transition from Pisces to Aquarius.

95. 7.12.41 The work of the Mysteries and dedication thereto in support of the principles for which we are fighting.

96. 14.12.41 The rising tide of evolution.

97. 21.12.41 Contact with the Masters.

98. 11.1.42 The spiritual principles of the New Age.

99. 18.1.42 The spiritual principles of efficiency.

100. 25.1.42 The power and practice of sympathetic magic.

101. 1.2.42 "The statesman must be more than an expression of what is living in his people. Much will depend on whether at the critical moment the world is ready for the leadership of the men of vision." (Quotation from the Dutch Premier, Dr Gorbrandy, in *Sunday Times* interview.)

102. 8.2.42 The visible fulcrum of power.

103. 15.2.42 The visible fulcrum of power.

104. 22.2.42 The rising Aquarian tide.

105. 1.3.42 The opening of the doors of the House of Nations.

106. 8.3.42 The seeking of the servants of truth to lead the nation.

107. 15.3.42 The overruling influence of the higher principles.

108. 22.3.42 The new tides.

109. 29.3.42 Spiritual integrity.

110. 5.4.42 The new leaders of the New Age, and their guidance by the Cosmic Plan.

111. 12.4.42 The solution of the Indian problem in the light of cosmic principles.

112. 19.4.42 Knowledge and understanding.

113. 26.4.42 The service of the Masters.

114. 3.5.42 The rising tide of the new life.

115. 10.5.42 Letting bygones be bygones.

116. 17.5.42 A new spirit in human affairs.

117. 24.5.42 The danger indicated in this letter.

118.   31.5.42   The possibility of having to change our way of living for the sake of social justice.

119.   7.6.42   The power of concentrated thought, used in group formation, to bring spiritual ideals into manifestation.

120.   14.6.42   The calling of Arthur.

121.   21.6.42   Dedication to the higher unity.

122.   28.6.42   The new man in the New Age.

123.   5.7.42   The reality of the powers with which we are working.

124.   12.7.42   The intuition of God's will for man.

125.   19.7.42   The coming of the Aquarian Age.

126.   26.7.42   The illumination of the mass mind.

127.   2.8.42   The illuminated mass mind of the nation.

128.   9.8.42   The ideals behind the plan.

129.   16.8.42   The need for self-discipline and self-sacrifice in the working of democracy.

130.   23.8.42   Let each one of us make of his own life a nucleus from which the new life can begin to spread.

131.   30.8.42   The true leadership of the nation.

132.   6.9.42   Dedicated leadership.

133.   12.9.42   The formation of a nucleus of spiritual chivalry.

134.   20.9.42   True leadership is service of the led.

135.   27.9.42   The critical examination of religion and ethics with reference to the needs of the New Age.

136.   4.10.42   The nucleus of dedicated and initiated.

INDEX

CPSIA information can be obtained at www.ICGtesting.com
Printed in the USA
LVOW042144110312

272609LV00007B/1/P